Rise, Shine, Be Woke

Anita Coleman
Stephanie Patterson
Francena Willingham
Ash Coleman
Marvella Lambright
Susan Skoglund
Sharon Wakamoto

Charis Research
Irvine, California
2018

Set in Times New Roman and Bodoni MT Black

Published by Charis Research
PO Box 50422, Irvine, CA 92619
Email: casa.charis.@gmail.com

Library of Congress Control Number: 2018901559

ISBN: 0989663167
ISBN-13: 978-0-9896631-6-8

DEDICATION

Woke (noun) means being aware of race, racism, racialization, and how the concept of race keeps mutating to create new injustices.

Race is an evil concept. Embedded deeply in the psyche, culture, society and institutions of the USA racism, predates race.
Racism cannot be easily eradicated.

This book is dedicated to all who are working to end racism.

CONTENTS

RISE, SHINE, BE WOKE

HOW TO USE THIS BOOK

Individuals:

- **Read the stories**. Allow them to raise questions that expand your understanding of racialization. For example, how do your memories of the early 2000s compare with that of the immigrant woman? What do you remember about learning or growing up during segregation or integration?
- **Study, Survey, Shine.** Dip into the Glossary. Go online regularly to the Anti-racism Digital Library, http://endracism.info.
- **Wake up the world around you.** Gift the book to a friend or family member. Encourage your local school, public, and church libraries to add this book to their collection.

Groups:

- **Book group reading.** Select the book for your group; a guide is included at the end of book.
- **Plan forums and panels**. Invite one or more of the writers, or similar local people, to tell their stories and create language that helps end racism. Ask questions: Is representation without racialization possible? How do skin color labels perpetuate racism? What is American identity?
- **Hold Courageous Conversations**. Organize bold talks and link them to a Call for Action. Use legacy or culture sharing, gaming, story-telling, and interactive, real-time engagement with anti-racism and diversity resources from the Anti-racism Digital Library, http://endracism.info.

ACKNOWLEDGMENTS

At the Fall 2017 meeting of the Board of Directors of Presbyterian Women, Inc. Francena Willingham led a community building activity. At her request, the women formed small groups and shared three of their shining moments in life. Over and over again, they were stories of faith, family, and education. I was so impressed by what I heard that I invited the women to contribute their stories for a book. In keeping with the 2018 PW Gathering theme of Arise, Shine, Your Light Has Come, the book would be titled: *Rise, Shine, Be Woke.*

Stephanie was one of the first to send her story and over the next few months she kept them coming despite Advent, Christmas, and a battle with pneumonia! Francena too sent her story promptly. I invited my son, a young millennial man. Ash graciously offered two essays. I donated my editing and publishing expertise and brought the first proof copy for review to the Spring 2018 PW Board meeting. Upon return from the March, Spring Board meeting, another board member, Marvella Lambright sent her story. From my Synod of Southern California and Hawaii, I invited Susan Skoglund and Sharon Wakamoto. They too shared.

What you hold in your hands now is a result of that spontaneity. Without the generous sharing of these folks this book would not have come into being. I applaud my co-authors and PW, Inc. for a nurturing environment in which such creative work can emerge so organically and informally.

Not everything was smooth sailing. The book faced challenges. On March 20th I was led to use my voice when people without homes in my County were being stereotyped. I wanted to change the tone of the Not-In-My-Backyard rhetoric. As I engaged, it became obvious that many people were homeless because of economic uncertainty and housing shortages; class prejudices, which are inseparable from racism, was also playing a role whereby good people were unwittingly criminalizing the poor. When over 300 residents joined my advocacy to the City Mayor this became a community education and engagement initiative. Extending grace to learn and change our attitudes we began empowering each other to figure out inclusion in the polarizing arena of housing.

On 18th March, two days before the homelessness crisis that would take me away from the book for the next two months, I received Francena's revision, plus family photos. On June 18th I decided to include her photos in the book. I was feeling good the next morning of the 19th as the book was back on track finally. PW Board Chair Carol Winkler's email later that day was a shock: Francena was dead. June 18th was also the third anniversary of the 2015 Charleston Church shooting. Sleepless, I browsed emails, looked at pictures I'd taken of Francena, and made a short video. I was comforted by two quotes in the signature line of her last email to me:

Faith is the substance of things *hoped* for, the evidence of things not seen. Hebrews 11:1

"The only journey is the one within." - Rainer Maria Rilke

I pray that *Rise, Shine, Be Woke* will nurture faith, inspire shining moments, and rich journeys. May the stories light our way to be transformative, integrative anti-racists building a shared community of equals who serve each other.

Anita Coleman, Irvine, California
First written February 24
Last updated July 7, 2018

In Memoriam

Francena Willingham, Ph. D.

Francena Willingham, passed away on June 18th in her home at 3417 Carver Street, Columbia, South Carolina. Born on October 5, 1949, in Greenbriar, she was the daughter of the late Frank Willingham, Jr. and Mary Mitchell Willingham. She was an educator and administrator who taught mathematics in Richland County School Districts One and Two, the Jasper County School District and as a professor at both Benedict and Morris Colleges.

Surviving family include her brother, Elliott Willingham, Sr. (Lydia) of Columbia, SC, her aunt Gertrude Mitchell of Washington, D.C., nephew Elliott Willingham, Jr. (Priscilla) of Charlotte, NC, niece Renee Willingham Gilbert (James) of West Lafayette, Indiana, one grandnephew and two grandnieces along with a host of relatives and friends.

We love you. We will never forget you. And, we promise to Rise, Shine, Be Woke.

LEADING EDGE BABY BOOMERS: FROM SEGREGATION TO COMMUNITY

Leading edge baby boomers are people born between the years of 1945 and 1954. The defining point is that they came of age during the Vietnam War.

Susan Skoglund shares about growing up during segregation in Texas, experiencing diversity in California, and acknowledging white privilege.

Growing up in segregated South Carolina, Marvella Lambright recounts how she and other 6-year olds found a way to be together.

Francena Willingham's memoir chronicles her lineage, culture, journey and many shining moments as an educator in the Deep South.

Sharon Wakamoto explains the role of faith in her life and how belonging to Presbyterian Women has nurtured her to become the person God created her to be.

Susan Skoglund

From Growing Up Segregated to Experiencing Diversity and Acknowledging White Privilege

Like many others of my generation (I turned 75 in May), I grew to adulthood very conscious of the civil rights struggle. I was a product of Texas segregated schools, neighborhoods and churches. I took for granted my place in society and had no idea about white privilege. I grew up in a hill country community filled with German immigrants. I was born during World War II and despite our German heritage, my paternal grandfather served as County sheriff. During my high school and college years, I had an increasing awareness that segregation was wrong and that people of color and African Americans in particular were treated very unfairly and with great prejudice. I married an Air Force officer and for the next 20 years or so continued to live in a very white world still unaware of the advantages that gave me.

In 1987, we were assigned to a base in Southern California. I entered the workforce as a civil servant and found a wonderful world of diversity with colleagues and friends of many ethnicities. I learned how cheated I had been in my segregated world. I learned so much from my peers of color. They helped me better understand the diverse public with whom we worked. I observed how better equipped they were to handle disappointment and withstand adversity. I was able to grow more resilient following their examples. As my career progressed I continued to benefit from this diversity. I particularly remember a staff meeting in which I first introduced a new idea for consideration. It was only taken seriously after a white male took the ideas as his own and reintroduced it. It was my male African American colleague who was quick to assert that it was my idea originally. Thank you, Frank! I think about how beneficial it would have been to have been more open to my schoolmates of Mexican heritage and to have had African American students with us as well. My life could have been so much richer.

After retirement and growing more active in Presbyterian Women, my awareness grew. I learned that some of my Japanese PW sisters had been forced to live in internment camps in Arizona during World War II. The injustice of this and the irony of how different it had been for my German family added fuel to my growing enlightenment that the position I occupied in life resulted from white privilege rather than my abilities and charm! I had access to better schools, easier access to home ownership which increases financial growth and stability, freedom from fear of authority among many other advantages. I served on the Churchwide Coordinating Team from 2009 – 2012 which gave me the opportunity to serve on its Anti-racism Committee. This expanded my knowledge and consciousness exponentially. I continue to do what I can to work against racism and increase acknowledgment of white privilege and systemic racism.

Marvella Lambright

Segregation Would Not Allow Us To Be Together in Plain Sight, But We Found A Way!

The first time I remember racism touching my life was as a girl in 1955 in Charleston, SC. I was 6 years old. The street I lived on was very narrow with a clear line between whites and Negroes, as blacks were referred to at that time. One side of the street had a segregated white trailer park and the other side had blacks who owned modest houses. The people on the street DID NOT interact. The Ku Klux Klan did still ride through the street after dark. We turned out our lights, as not to be noticed.

The children of the two sides of the street would stand or sit on the curb of each side and talk across the street to each other. I knew how to do hand sewing with a needle and thread for my doll. The little white girls wanted to know how to do it too. I would run across the street and give them a quick short lesson. Then, when we thought no one was looking. One of them would run across to me and my friend, Sandra for a sewing lesson. Then one of us would run over to them. This went on all summer. My father absolutely forbade us from being with the white children across the street. Then we all

4

started first grade in segregated schools.

Segregation would not allow us to be together in plain sight. However, we found a way to be together that summer.

When school desegregation began in 1964, I was one of the first to go to the local high school in the first integrated class. I later went on to South Carolina State College to become a Home Economics Teacher, teaching cooking and SEWING to all races of children!

Francena Willingham

My Lineage, Born To Teach

As an African American baby boomer, I was born four years after the end of World II, where my father, Frank Willingham, Jr. (1915-1966), served patriotically. I was named for him and my birthplace was Greenbrier, South Carolina near Winnsboro, SC. However, when my father returned to the United States, African Americans were still subjected to the harsh reality of Jim Crow. Segregation and ill treatment of blacks continued to be pernicious, and still ruled the day.

Two years after the World War II, my parents were married in her parents' house. My brother and my only sibling was born 11 months and 3 weeks after me; that qualifies us to be Irish twins. Both the maternal and paternal sides of my family did not accept the culture of the day without their own familial protest. My mother's father, Allen Cisero Mitchell (1892-1968) refused to allow his three daughters and son to serve as domestic workers. His children had to work their own garden and sell the wares to the neighbors which included whites. Allen's brother, Robert (1888-1944), became an A.M.E. Zion Bishop who finished Livingston College and vowed to send my grandfather to college. Instead, he married very soon after graduating. Hence, Robert never fulfilled that promise.

Starling Glenn (1823?), my maternal great-great grandfather, was owned by Jerimiah Glenn, a rich Presbyterian who believed in educating blacks. Jerimiah later gave Starling his freedom and heritage. Starling's son, John Benjamin Glenn (1849-1892), was my maternal great-grandfather, who was taught to read by his slave master; and, he attended Biddle University, currently known as Johnson C. Smith University. John was given his freedom at age 12. He was a teacher and an A.M.E. minister. John completed his education at Benedict College in Columbia, SC. His wife was my maternal great-grandmother, Mary McConnell Glenn (1859-1935), who literally helped lay down the foundation to the family church, Shiloh Presbyterian Church (U.S.A.), in Winnsboro, SC. My maternal grandmother, Carrie Lou Glenn Mitchell (1892-1957), was a well-respected licensed teacher who loved math. All four of her children finished Historically Black Colleges and Universities (HBCU): one from Livingston College, Salisbury, North Carolina; two from Johnson C. Smith University, Charlotte, NC; and, one from A & T University, Greensboro, NC.

My mother, Mary Jane Mitchell Willingham (1922-2008), had three majors while in college at Johnson C. Smith University: Mathematics, History, and French. Her first teaching job was at Carver School in Columbia, SC. During the summers, my mother worked at Gimbrells Department store in New York City by pretending to be a French Moroccan. At the time African Americans could not be store clerks, even in New York City. Finally, in 1950 my maternal grandmother, Carrie, graduated from Allen University, an HBCU in Columbia, SC, after all of her children had done so. To her credit, all of her children eventually attained Master's Degrees.

My paternal grandfather, Frank Willingham (1866-1964), accumulated close to 500 acres of land, rented houses, gave land for a school in the community, and had his own workers. His father, Thomas, my great-great grandfather, married a Blackfoot Native American, Sylvia Gibson (Ellison) (1842-1946). He lived and died in Anderson, South Carolina.

My father, Frank Jr., owned a store and had a pulp wood business. His brother, Booker T., migrated to Detroit during the Great Migration to work in the General Motors plant. While on a visit at home, he was stopped by police and given a speeding ticket because he was driving a Buick Roadmaster. He told them to go ahead and give him two tickets because he would be returning in the same manner. On his way back, they attempted to stop him again. But he outran them on the back roads. He did not return until the funeral of his father.

Another brother, Nathaniel (1905-1988) had a son who became the first black collegiate football coach, Tyrone Willingham (1953-), for a major university, Stanford. Other cities that the Willingham siblings migrated to included: Jacksonville, NC, Baltimore, MD, New York City, Philadelphia, PA, and Washington, D.C.

Finally, my paternal grandmother, Alice Clark Willingham (1888-1950), raised her five orphaned sisters and brothers; and, her nephew, Dr. James R. Clark (1937-1979), became an Internist and an expert on sickle cell anemia. He was one of the founders of the Columbia Area Sickle Cell Anemia Foundation which bears his name today. Because of these stories, I have always believed that I would excel and I did not cultivate a feeling of inferiority to the current majority race of America. These stories have helped shaped my ethos. I always knew that I would attend college. It was expected. However, as the first grandchild on my maternal side, I was showered with many toys. I remember my maternal uncle, Allen (1921-2010) and his wife, giving me a doll with brown skin. I ran away and cried. To this day, I have no clue as to why I reacted in that manner. Was it subconscious?

The watershed moment for me realizing the vestiges of segregation happened the first time I rode the Columbia city bus. At the age of 8, I accompanied an out of town family friend to shop downtown. I just sat down at the front of the bus. The driver rudely told me to move behind the white line. I was oblivious to why at the time. However, it was etched into my memory. Also, at this age, my parents became legally separated.

I grew up in Ladson Presbyterian Church (U.S.A) in Columbia, SC, where I have attended and have been a member since moving to Columbia. It is an historical black church that started in 1838. The members first worshiped in the galleries of First Presbyterian Church of Columbia, SC. While at Ladson, I have served as moderator of both the Diaconate and Presbyterian Women. Additionally, I was elected an elder in 1998 and I have served as treasurer of the Sunday School. On the Presbytery, Synod, and Church-wide levels for Presbyterian Women, I have served in various positions. My faith always and continues to sustain me.

My formal education began in Columbia, SC. I attended the Drew Park Kindergarten while we lived with the Vance family near this school. My father stayed in Greenbrier and we boarded with the Vances during the week. At the same time, our new house was being built in the Booker T. Washington Heights of Columbia, SC. This was an area of the city where many of my father's relatives resided, including two maternal uncles. The residents were middle and working-class blacks that owned their homes. After a visit by the well-known black educator, Booker T. Washington, the community honored him with its name. After leaving Drew Park, I was allowed to enter first grade before the deadline to turn six at Sarah Nance Elementary School. Mr. Burton, the brother of Mrs. Vance, was the principal. By the summer before 5th grade, my mother had taught me all the math required for that grade. Hence, the teacher would always send me on errands because I would always finish my math work before all the other students. I enjoyed this freedom to roam the halls.

My Junior High school years (7th and 8th grades) were spent at W.A. Perry. I became a member of the Junior Honor Society and the Library Club. However, I did not remain there for my 9th grade year, I entered Booker T. Washington High School (BTW) in Columbia, SC. Mother had purchased me a clarinet while in Junior High. She wanted me to play in the Marching 100 Band of BTW where she taught math and served as the department's chair. Our band director applied every year for us to march in the Macy's Thanksgiving Parade. It never happened. However, we did get the invitation to march in the 1964 Cherry Blossom Parade of Washington D.C. I can remember it like it was yesterday. We marched down Pennsylvania Avenue. We also visited the DC tourist sites. When we arrived at the Washington Monument, several of us were too late to ride up in elevator. That did not deter us. We were going to the top. Hence, we ran up and down over 900 steps each way to do so. Ah! To be young. All of my teachers were black except for the innovation of Educational Television (ETV). In the 8th grade, South Carolina History was taught on this medium and teacher was white; also, it was devoid of any topics on slavery. Often times when our regular teacher would leave the classroom during the broadcast, the class clown would turn the channel to cartoons and the teacher never was aware. We did not tell. Additionally, during my ninth-grade year at BTW, we had Algebra I and Physical Science taught by ETV, and the teachers were white. The Physical Science teacher had a deformed hand. However, we did not make fun of him like the current POTUS, Donald Trump. We were from a different thought paradigm.

Next, in the summer of 1966, I attended an English program that helped boost my verbal SAT score. The program was managed by Harvard University and our teachers were of the Caucasian persuasion. This was also the year that my father died in a one car accident in St. Mathews, SC. The police said that he fell asleep at the wheel at 6:30 in the morning. My mother never believed the story. She thought that the police had something to do with his demise. When they were together, mother recalled to me a court case initiated by my father against a white man who had given him poor service. Hence, he refused to pay him. The judge ruled against him. However, my father still did not pay the white man. The town's people knew that my father had an account in the local bank. And this bank had the effrontery to take the money owed to the white man out of my father's account, without his approval. My father and his family were not afraid of the power structure. They would take them to task. However, he did close his account with that bank.

Even though my father and mother had been legally separated for over 8 years, she kept an insurance policy on him because they never divorced. Her brother, Allen, was a Funeral Home Director and he cautioned all his sisters to maintain an insurance policy on their husbands. Mother arranged the funeral to occur in the family church of Morris Creek Baptist in Winnsboro, SC.

Again, while at BTW, I was in the Honor Society, served on the student council, voted most likely to succeed, held the office of president of the class of 1967, and graduated first in my class. However, I was not called valedictorian because that person was voted on by the class to be the speaker at commencement. The school changed the rules so that the valedictorian would truly be someone who could speak. My rank allowed me to compete for the title, but, I did not win.

I attended Talladega College, an HBCU, on a full scholarship in 1967 because of my SAT scores. The scholarship was named for one of its founders, William Savery. He along with Thomas Tarrant and Ambrose Headen began the school in Talladega, Alabama in 1867. All of them had been enslaved. I majored in mathematics and physics. While pledging a sorority in the fall of my sophomore year, I almost failed my first Physics course. By the end of the semester, I brought the grade up to a "B." Yet, I had no fear of losing my scholarship because it could not be taken away due to poor grades. That was one reason I accepted it instead of going to Johnson C. Smith University or Blackburn College.

On the weekends, buses from the Birmingham community would arrive on campus for us to participate in demonstration marches. I would hop on the bus to go to Birmingham. Also, speakers like Stokely Carmichael would often visit our campus. During the summers, while at Talladega, I worked at Camps Burnt Gin and Mill Creek in Wedgefield and Pineville

South Carolina, respectively. These camps were for
orthopedic children who were in wheel chairs or had
prosthesis. One young boy had lost all his limbs except one
hand. Yet, he could swim like a fish. All of the children
were well adjusted. I certainly learned from this job to always
be grateful of what you have. Immediately, after graduating
college with a 3.7 grade point average, I accepted a fellowship
from Washington University in St. Louis, MO, where I
obtained the M.A.T. degree in mathematics in 1972.

My first math teaching job was at Dreher High School, in
Columbia, SC. Even though a current Math Education
professor at the University of Illinois believes that teaching
math is white privilege. I have a spoiler alert. I guess I broke
the glass ceiling when I taught both advanced placement
courses of Algebra II and Geometry at Dreher. Geometry was
my favorite subject at BTW; and, achieving all "A's" in this
course helped me to graduate first in my class of over 300
students. Even though BTW was closed in 1974, Dreher
continues to be a majority school, in Columbia, SC. Later, I
was selected at Dreher to teach Math in the first state piloted
Academically Creative and Talented (ACT) Program. It
offered a tailored curriculum for the gifted and talented
population. I have also taught at W.J. Kennan High School
and Blythewood Academy in Columbia. Additionally, I was
recognized in the 1979 edition of the ***Book of Honor***;
recognized in the tenth edition of ***Personalities of the South***;
and, listed in the 1972 edition of ***Outstanding Young Women
of America***.

Several times I traveled as a chaperone to Europe and
Asia during Spring Break with students. By 1981, bitten by
the administration bug, I moved to the Low Country of South
Carolina, specifically, Jasper County. I became a vice
principal at West Hardeeville High School in Hardeeville, and
then acting principal, and the Chapter 1 Supervisor of
Mathematics, Reading and Readiness.

However, I became restless again, and I decided to pursue
a terminal degree at Iowa State University in 1986. I was

awarded a minority graduate assistantship to pursue my studies. By 1990, I had worked diligently to attain a Ph.D. in Educational Administration. I published and copyrighted my dissertation theses entitled: *The Development and Validation of an Instrument to Measure Selected Support Staff's Perception of School Climate.*

In the late summer of 1990, I arrived back in Columbia, and accepted an Associate Professor position at Benedict College. My title was the Director of the Armed Forces Teacher Education for Retirees (AFTER) Program. It was funded by The Coca Cola Foundation for two years. The mission of the program was to target the recruitment of minority military males and other mid-career professionals, holding bachelor's degrees, for teacher licensure in Elementary or Mathematics (Secondary). Another goal of the program was to increase the number of teachers from diverse backgrounds to serve as positive role models. To extend the program for an additional four years, I wrote a grant proposal to the FORD Foundation. We received conditional funding along with four other HBCUs: Bethune Cookman College, Daytona Beach, FL, Claflin College, Orangeburg, SC, St. Augustine College, Raleigh, NC, and Tugaloo College, Tugaloo, AL. We all targeted the military for teaching. It was administered by the United Negro College Fund.

During this period, I wrote several articles in refereed journals on the program. We also organized and coordinated the *Taste for Teaching Conference* hosted by Benedict College and sponsored the *New Teacher Recruitment and Retention Project of Teachers College, Columbia University*, in April 1993. We had over forty participants to receive teacher certification from the program. In 2015, Sharon Billue, a former participant who became a math teacher and had served in the Air Force, was selected the *Teacher of the Year* for Lexington School District 1 in Lexington SC. Additionally, she was a runner-up for the state title.

During my tenure at Benedict College, I presented many workshops to professional organizations on our programmatic thrusts; and, I do believe the ***Call Me MISTER Program*** of a Clemson University, in Clemson, SC, germinated from our program at Benedict College as a result of a presentation and our involvement in the South Carolina Association of Teacher Educators (SCATE) Conference in 1994. As they say, *"Imitation is the highest form of flattery."*

After retiring in 2011, my passion has been to read books on the antebellum south, the Civil War period, and the enslavement of blacks. In 2015, when the killings occurred at Emanuel AME church in Charleston, SC, I responded to an insensitive Facebook post with facts on the confederate battle flag and slavery; and, I also included references. To my astonishment, I had over 300 likes!

My mission now is to share this knowledge and help educate young blacks and others on the history of African Americans. I continue to be a teacher and servant/leader to help all to know the forgotten and untold history of blacks. Hopefully, comity and love of all the races will become the rule of the day.

My favorite quote, is from Robert Smalls (1839-1915), a former black congressman, when he uttered the following words at the 1895 South Carolina constitution convention:

> "My race needs no special defense, for the past history of them in this country proves them to be the equal of any people. All they need is an equal chance in the battle of life."

This quote is also inscribed on a monument at his burial site. Smalls served in both houses of the South Carolina legislature and two terms in the US House of Representatives during the Reconstruction Era.

Another favorite quote of mine is, "The heights of great men reached and kept were not attained by sudden flight, but they, while their companions slept, were toiling upward in the night," by Henry Wadsworth Longfellow. We all need to

Rise, Shine, Be Woke!

Left: Francena maternal grandmother Carrie Lou Glenn Mitchell's 1950 college graduation picture,

Above: Francena's 1971 graduation from Talladega College, Talladega, AL.

Below: Family photo at Francena's 1990 Ph.D. graduation from Iowa State University, Ames, Iowa.

Above: Francena's paternal grandmother, Alice Clark
Willingham, Aunt Rosetta,
and Uncle Booker T.

Below: Francena Willingham (1949-2018) at age 2, and
mother Mary J.M. Willingham (1922-2008)

**From The State (Columbia, SC newspaper), July 5, 2018,
Four suspicious fires worry Columbia neighborhood:**

On June 18th, 2018, the Columbia Fire Dept. responded to a
fire and found Francena had died before the fire started. This
was the fourth suspicious fire in two months. Although the
other houses were unoccupied, the fires are making neighbors
fearful. The neighborhood is changing to renters and absentee
landlords. The Carver Elementary, W.A. Perry Middle, and
Booker T. Washington High schools are still highly ranked.

[President of the Booker Washington Heights Neighborhood
Association] Williams said Francena Willingham respected
Booker Washington Heights and wouldn't let go of the pride
the community once knew. Willingham's father laid the
stones that built her house in 1960, Williams told City
Council, and even though her brother pleaded with her to
move, Willingham chose to stay. "Living in that
neighborhood, she knew the importance of maintaining that
history," Williams says. She loved where she lived.

Below: Francena's home for most of her life.

Sharon Wakamoto

Nurtured By Presbyterian Women to Become the Person God Created Me to Be

Presbyterian Women, Inc. (PW) has had a major influence on my life for almost 20 years. Previous to that most of my time in the Lord's work was at Placentia Presbyterian Church where my husband Chuck and I had become members in 1968. Outside the church, my only other Christian ministry experience was with the fund raising auctions of the Mary Magdalene Project, a ministry begun by Presbyterian Women to help street prostitutes. This is where I first met my first PW women: Jerri Rodewald and Shari Stump.

After retiring from teaching in 2000, my involvement in Los Ranchos Presbytery Committee on the Preparation for Ministry (CPM) sparked my Christian journey. The six years on CPM served as a springboard to involvement in the Synod of Southern California and Hawaii and the beginning of my PW connection. Jo Smith and I had served on the Synod Personnel Committee together. She invited me to be a part of the Mission Committee of the Los Ranchos Presbytery Coordinating Team of PW, called the PWP CT. The PWP CT is the group of women leaders from different churches in the presbytery. PWP CT then had similar positions to what we have today such as Moderator, Vice-Moderator for Mission, Vice Moderator for Justice and Peace, and Members at Large for Asian American Women, Hispanic Women, Justice and Peace, etc. From these beginnings I came to know wonderful Presbyterian women, near and far. Jo Smith and Marilyn Johnson were my earliest mentors as they got me more involved with PW. Beyond my presbytery, in the Synod, I saw how much more active Jerri and Shari from the Mary Magdalene project were in PW. Involvement with PW ministries such as Fellowship of the Least Coin, United States of America Mission Experience, and the Global Exchange expanded my awareness too in two significant ways. One, it showed me another dimension of Christian friendship. I realized how much I had missed out in not having this kind of Christian women nurture earlier in my life. Two, I became more aware of the injustices towards women and children in the OC (Orange County, California) and around the world.

At the time when PWP came into my life, the only PW group at my church was the Martha Circle mostly comprised of faithful senior women. I did not join the group but loved the women and would take some of them to the PWP Gatherings. Now, we have a Horizons Bible Study group that meets monthly on Saturdays followed by lunch at a local restaurant. Our church PW (PWC) group is known as the Women of Faith. Next year, our Bible study leader will be a member of the presbytery PW leadership, PWP CT. The first PW ministry started in my church was fair trade coffee. Because of PW, we began to purchase fair trade. Initially, we only served fair trade during coffee time after Sunday worship but soon, it was made available for purchase too. That I could do my little bit, in an everyday way, to help someone, somewhere, made a difference to me.

I am at the stage where my faith is the most important thing in my life. I have never been one who needs role models to look like me. Rather, I have always admired anyone who uses the gifts they have been by God to utmost fulfillment and becoming the person God created them to be. The PW purpose upon which its ministries rest have layer upon layer of faith, mission, and servant leadership, which nurtures women in an inclusive, caring community of women of faith who strengthen the church and witness to the promise of God's kingdom. I am grateful for the rich friendships and diverse experiences given to me because of PW.

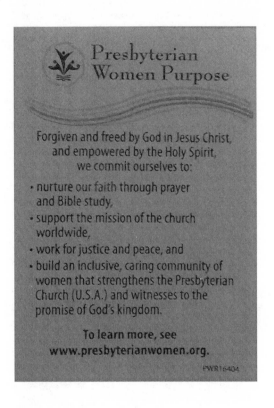

A BABY BUSTER: FROM INTEGRATION TO INCLUSION

Baby busters, also known as Generation X, are the 13th Generation of Americans, people who were born between 1965 to 1980. This is at least a decade and more after the 1954 historic ruling of BROWN V. BOARD OF EDUCATION which desegregated public schools in the USA. **Stephanie Patterson Morris** sketches her memories of integration poignantly. In essays that probe her culture and history she reveals how self-confidence, resilience, and her strong anti-racist identity developed.

Stephanie Patterson

I Was Right

From as early as I can remember, I always knew I was different. I was raised by my great grandparents. That was different. As a child, I would shun playing outside with my friends because I would rather read a book. That was different. I would strive for perfection, not because I was being made to, but because it was my desire. That was different. I never wanted to be like anyone other than myself. I always felt that being different would help me stand out in the crowd. It would help me to see life as God intended and would help me to love and appreciate diversity. Being different would allow me to appreciate diversity and empower others to love themselves and achieve greatness. I always believed being different was good. I was wrong.

In September of 1975, I was one of many children in Jefferson County, Kentucky who was exposed to integration via cross-district busing. I have always, even then, had a vast love of education, so I remember being excited about the exposure to new and different people and learning opportunities as I entered 3rd grade. I had skipped a few grades in school, so was always younger than my classmates. I remember feeling scared about not being within walking distance from my home; about being so far away from my great grandparents.

Figure 1: Jefferson County Public School buses damaged by protesters.

As I traveled to school aboard the large yellow school bus, we were close to my new elementary school, when the bus suddenly flipped on its side into a ditch on the right side of the two-lane road. Hearing the other children wail and cry from being hurt, I wanted to cry too. But I couldn't. I guess I was in shock. After the authorities came and rescued us, we were transported to school by other vehicles. Some students were taken to the hospital, others were not. I am unsure how the determination was made on who should go and who shouldn't. I later found out the cause of the crash was due to a car that ran us off the road. Our bus was attacked by a person or persons who strongly opposed desegregation and wanted to make sure that we, black students, weren't able to learn alongside their white children. I was just a child. Why was I hated so much? Why were people so afraid to allow me equal access to a quality education? That was my first negative experience of being different, but definitely not my last.

Throughout my life I have always had to achieve over and above just to be even considered equal to others. They want what's in my mind, but not the package in which the knowledge is delivered. A battle I still fight today and I assume for the remainder of my life. Yes, at times I grow weary, but I'll never give up or give in. Whenever I feel like I cannot continue this path, I hear the voice of my great grandmother saying, "I believe in you. People can take many things away from you, but your education is not one of them. They can never take away your knowledge. God placed you on this earth for a reason." I find myself repeating those words not only to my children, but to others as well. I use being different as a way to encourage others to absorb as much knowledge as possible. When I began work on my doctorate degree, I was asked by many why I wanted to achieve that degree. My reply was because it is my responsibility. There are so many minorities, females, and others that have the desire and the ability to achieve that level of education; since I am able, it is my responsibility to do so and be the example for others. I need to be the example for my children, my grandchildren, my nieces and nephews, and other children who desperately need to see someone who looks like them, someone different, making great achievements.

I never wanted to be like anyone other than myself. I always felt that being different would help me stand out in the crowd. It would help me to see life as God intended and would help me to love and appreciate diversity. Being different would allow me to appreciate diversity and empower others to love themselves and achieve greatness. I always believed being different was good. I was right.

Stephanie Patterson

We Are, Therefore I Am

Worship has arguably been described as the epitome of faith. As a child growing up in the African American community, when worship was discussed, faith had no choice but to enter the conversation and vice versa. The journey of faith and African American worship has continually been loaded with much emotion; an ongoing journey with a ubiquitous impact on our lives. Regardless of denomination, African American Christians engaged in worship have several commonalities. Two of them being the sharing of a historical reality, based on struggle and survival, and the offering of praise and thanksgiving.

Africa, an unknown land to Western-oriented Christians, was an obvious target of attack because of its vast natural resources, its creatively skilled and sturdy inhabitants, and their development of the world's basics of survival, e.g., family structure, medicine, architecture, etc.

Even though the people of Africa were stripped of their culture, their empires, and their families, the slave traders could not take away the communal spirit that lived deep inside.

Western-oriented Christians believed Africans to be ignorant heathens. This belief widened the division between

African and European American worshipers. Colonial Christians did not want to share the message of freedom to slaves, so they propagated a distorted form of Christianity, one that would cause an act of compliance and would reveal the slave's new Christian state of being a "good" slave. Due to the birth of children and the importation of more slaves, the African American population increased and legislation allowed European Americans to place African Americans into three categories: political, economic, and cultural. Africans were seen as slaves or prisoners of all European American society. They were seen as property, similar to cattle and were thought of as "overgrown and witless children, lost heathens in need of salvation, and fearful, untrustworthy, but fascinating and often desirable sensual savages whose African roots would soon wither away" (Costen, 2007).

Many rituals of African religion were banned, including drums, dancing, and even the rites of passage in death. Anything that European Americans did not understand or feared was declared "heathen" and a "pagan." The derogatory classifications also proved to be an attempt to purge African roots, eliminating history, and making the African people more dependent. For slave owners, this made enslavement more controllable. As more slaves turned to Western-oriented Christianity, colonists viewed it as an opportunity to use language to gain even more control. Narratives were produced and presented to adult slave candidates for baptism. They had wordings such as: "You declare…that you do not ask for the holy baptism out of any design to free yourself from the Duty and Obedience that you owe to your Master while you live…" (Costen, 2007). Slaves in some communities were forced to attend worship services, while in different communities, slaves were not allowed to attend. Slave narratives were abundant and inconsistent with slave masters who spoke of the liberation the gospel provided, but lived, as they did not believe. Christian fellowship never existed between slaves and their masters. The dugout pits created below the pulpit, by churches, to pack African Christians in for worship created true isolation.

As Africans in America learned to find meaning in the concepts present in the Bible, they began to build on the internalized spirit within them and create their own type of Christianity. Slaves created a sacred space where they were free to worship God their way. Water saturated quilts and blankets were hung to define the space for worship. A large black iron wash pot full of water would be placed in the center to muffle the sound of their voices. These types of secret meetings away from the slave masters would become known as part of the Invisible Institution. Although oppressed, slaves were free to give thanks and praise God wholeheartedly. Thus, African American worship was born. Praise and thanksgiving are of the utmost importance in the African American Christian community. "African peoples perceive reality as one related whole rather than as separate compartments" (Costen, 2007, ebook). A division between sacred and secular does not exist.

Early Americans of African descent and their ancestors were survivors. They desired freedom and only God could provide it so having a personal relationship with Christ was the goal. The only way to achieve a personal relationship with God is through prayer, so it was and still is a very important and large part of communal gatherings. Those gathered not only listen to the prayer leader but also vocally respond with prayers of thanksgiving. Verbal cadences ring out during prayer such as, "thank you, Jesus!"; "yes, Lord!" and "help us, Jesus!" Slave owners also believed in the effectiveness of prayer provided by the slaves. They would, at times, ask slaves to pray for immediate concerns they had. Whether the slave was in prayer for him or herself or his or her owner, the words, "the Lord's will be done" would also be included as slaves knew the outcome was ultimately in God's hands and God knew what was best.

"Worship," for African Americans, "is more experiential than rationalistic. Its focus is on the communal sharing of reality rather than simply the transmission of information." Rather than seeking to *know about* God from doctrines and creeds, as the Western-oriented Christian, African peoples desire[d] to *know* God on a personal level (Costen, 2007).

Singing is an artistic expression that is deeply rooted in African culture. It is through song and music that African Americans achieve a sense of closeness to God and God's presence. Through their daily struggle, the tougher times were, the closer slaves felt to God. Music allows imagination and understanding of oneself. According to W.E.B. DuBois, "music is the soul of Black Folks." That is why the Invisible Institution was so important to African Americans and their survival. They could continue to endure their harsh lives as long as they were able to communicate with God through worship (Harding, 1981, p. 29).

Today, there is a strong spiritual bond between African Americans and their ancestors. This is true even for those African Americans who may not consider themselves Christian and may have never attended a church service. The struggle, the pain, and the right to survive come out, through music and dance. Music such as the Blues, Gospel, and even Hip Hop and various forms of dance reflect the spirit of Africa; a spirit that has never died and cannot be deadened.

Even though there are differences in denominational styles of worship, for most African Americans through the strong bond of kinship, members across denominations do not feel out of place attending another African American church outside his or her own or even another African American church of a different denomination. Hospitality is ever-present in the African American culture striving to make all feel welcome when they enter the home or church home. Why? Because the glory of Jesus transcends all blood ties and is mandated in the Word to be in obedience to God's will (see Matthew 12:46–50, Mark 3:31–35, and Luke 8:19–21).

African American Worship is a way for Americans of African descent to remain connected to one another and to Christ. Through song, music, and dance, worshippers not only use imagery, but also words brought to life through stories and imagination. These tools provide hope and empowerment in dark situations, while allowing worshippers to remain connected with their ancestors of whom without them, we would not have survived. Simply stated, I AM because WE ARE and since WE ARE therefore I AM!

References

Costen, M. W. (2007). African-American Christian Worship (2nd ed.). Nashville, TN: Abingdon Press.

Stephanie Patterson

A Reflection Of Enslaved Africans' Encounter With Christianity

Receiving my K-12 education in the public-school system, I was taught that African Americans had no past, other than that of a slave. I was taught that we had absolutely nothing to be proud of and any race that was non-White were savages. We were only good at destruction and the only reason the race was allowed to survive was to perform hard labor. Even though advanced for our species, we were still animals. Some of us were also teachable through constant lessons of how to be civil from the white race. As I continued my education after high school and took it upon myself to take courses in Pan-American history, I was taught that Europeans stole Africans from their homeland and stripped and robbed them of their culture and heritage. A majority of the slaves were very docile beings that accepted their fate and made the best of a horrible situation. Christianity was something that was forced on slaves as a means to control slaves both physically and mentally. These prior taught beliefs were only partially true.

It is believed that Europeans are responsible for the brutal slave trade as we know it, but its beginnings did not start with sheer brutality. Africans sold Africans into slavery for goods.

They were brought to the new world as indentured servants with the expectation of being fed and housed for their work. Afterwards, they would be given "freedom dues," which commonly included a section of land and provisions.

Africans brought their culture and religion with them to the new world. Enslaved Africans had faith in the spirit world, believing the spirit influenced the physical. They had deep convictions in the guidance from their ancestors via rituals, festivals, and strong tribal family and ethnic relationships believing that religion permeates. Some Europeans believed so deeply in the faith Africans had, that in times of sickness in the European households, the enslaver would send for the Black clergy or the slave that exhibited great faith, to come and pray over their sick family member. Thus from 1619–1700, in the time of colonial slavery, enslavers did not attempt to evangelize enslaved Africans. In some cases, syncretism would take place. Blacks and Whites would worship together.

At the end of the revolution and the Colonial Period, frontier revivalism exploded in the South. Nearly 95% of Blacks were practicing slave religion. Even though Whites controlled the first black churches, it was the black church that made the choice to disconnect itself from African ways. Many Blacks chose free-will religions such as Baptist and Methodist denominations. Yet, from approximately 1770 through the 1800s, for various reasons, most enslaved Africans were not Christians. Europeans refused to evangelize their slaves because economic profitability was the top priority. Slaves had a heavy work schedule and getting the work done was the solitary focus of slave owners. Some believed that Africans were too brutish to evangelize. Others had the belief that baptism would emancipate their slaves making them too proud and rebellious.

The lack of slave evangelism was intensified with Eli Whitney's invention of the cotton gin. There was so much money tied up in slavery that slave owners were not interested in the souls of their slaves. This fact caused moral outrage between the Europeans causing most denominations to split.

The church was at odds about what the biblical scripture states about slavery. In order to keep slaves under control, churches began to teach *Genesis 9:25–27,* the curse of Hamm, as a basis of enslavement.

With the lack of evangelism, slaves began to interpret religion for themselves. African Americans are oral in nature, passing things down via stories instead of writing down information. The Bible, for slaves, became a storehouse of rhetoric. Unsupervised slaves became more creative with the Bible, developing types of worship such as concert prayer where everyone prays at the same time; experiential religion in which this conversion was thought of as an emotional release that finds possession in the hysteria of expression; and Negro spirituals which spoke of the promised land, a place of emancipation, escape, and freedom from pain and suffering. Slavery was a form of hell on earth, but through the use of interpretative religion, slaves regarded life as a pilgrimage with their eyes set upon the Promised Land where their free spirits were transcendent.

The story does not end with the above reflection. It is ongoing. The more I learn, the more I discover, and the hungrier I become. I hope this reflection causes you to explore history, don't just believe what you are told. Do some digging for yourselves to find the truth.

Empower yourselves.

Stephanie Patterson

Stand For Something Or Fall For Anything

According to the Encyclopedia of Ethics, the word ethics is derived from the symbol meaning Greek ēthos, and the Latin word, 'morality' refers to one's character, routine, and custom. "The two words are often used interchangeably or with rather uncertain differences as in the phrases "personal morality" and "professional ethics"" (Ethics & Morality, 2001). When asked to describe my personal ethics, my professional ethics or my religious ethics, I view them as one. I have many guidelines which I govern myself such as striving to avoid excessive anger, abstaining from the use of alcoholic drinks as a beverage, saying no to recreational drugs and always striving to show support to family and friends. Of all the guidelines by which I strive to govern myself, three in particular stand out above the rest; personal development, self-reliance and the ethic of reciprocity also known in Christianity as the Golden Rule, which declares that we are to treat others as we would want to be treated ourselves.

I have constantly strived for personal development. Even as a child, I remember studying hard to achieve the best possible grade on a test. I received my first 'B' when I was in the seventh grade and remember crying nearly a week while examining my notes wondering where I went wrong. I did not place pressure on myself because of any type of competition with my peers. I did not place pressure on myself because of fear of being punished at home; my great grandparents raised me and they were always very supportive and understanding. They were my biggest fans. I have always been a highly independent person and I placed high expectations on myself due to a hunger I have to be the best me possible.

Some use the word independent interchangeably with the word disciplined. I am not one of those persons but do think that these two skills work best if used simultaneously. Even though I have younger brothers and sisters, I was raised as an only child. If I failed to perform a given task, I had no siblings around me to place the blame. At the other end of the spectrum, if I needed help with something, I was left to figure it out myself. As the oldest of my siblings, I was seen as the one with all the answers. So, I became self-reliant at a very early age. Independence is a skill, a personal and professional ethic. Whether in school or in my career, my responsibility includes completion of assigned tasks and preparing assignments specific to given instruction and desired results.

The Golden Rule dates back centuries, but for those who may be unfamiliar with the decree, the more recent reincarnation several years ago was, WWJD: What Would Jesus Do?" If found in a situation which you could not determine wrong from right, you could begin to wrestle with the answer by asking yourself, "how would I feel if that were done to me?" or "how would I feel if someone said that to me?" etc. Would the latter provide a decision for you? Sometimes. In the event that it did not, it at least provided a springboard to a possible right direction. Some may think of the above as a religious ethic and deem some unable to fulfill the decree. I have been active in the church my entire life so may be slightly partial, but I not only find the above to be an ethic, but also a moral standpoint. Morality is something inherent to us all, both religious and secular. My great grandmother would always say to me, "if you don't stand for something, you will fall for anything! You need to believe in something, even if you are the only one who believes."

Everyone has a foundation on which they have built their moral code. My foundation is built on religious beliefs, spirituality, and internal reflection. Whether personal, professional or religious ethics, morality, integrity, principles or a different coined term you choose, to succeed in a positive manner, you need to know what you stand for. Don't wait until you have to make a tough decision to begin thinking about your values. Establish and begin to live your personal, professional and religious ethic now.

References

Becker, L. C. & Becker, C. B. (2001). *Encyclopedia of Ethics.* PW(Vol. 3.) Taylor & Francis.

A LEGAL ALIEN: FROM IMMIGRATION AND NATURALIZATION TO CITIZENSHIP

Anita Coleman is a first generation immigrant to the USA. Growing up with no race in India and experiencing racialization, Anita finally found her freedom in her identity as a follower of Jesus Christ. Re awakening she accepts herself as an alien and sojourner whose true citizenship is in heaven. Attention to faithful spiritual formation and her professional development keep her actively listening, seeing beyond the social construction of race, to the essence of all humanity as imago Dei (made in God's image), and as one human race.

Anita Coleman

The "Other"

I came to America in the summer time with two suitcases, stars in my eyes, and my head filled with dreams. Isn't that how most immigrant stories begin?

I can still see myself in my mind's eye: A petite girl who looked far younger than she was clutching a suitcase that was tied up with a bright blue Kuwaiti Airways headset's electric cord. You see, the airline stewards, and they were all men - I don't recall seeing any women on the flight serving as stewardesses - had found my bag on the layover in Kuwait. They were unable to identify to whom it belonged; halfway into the journey which had started the night before, from Madras, India, the tags and labels had fallen off. So, the men had broken open the lock to make sure that it did not contain a bomb. When I came back to the plane I found the broken suitcase, its contents, which I can't remember now but I suspect were clothes, spilling out. My first thought remained with me for the rest of the flight: How was I going to carry it off the plane? There was nothing that could hold the suitcase closed. Inside, a storm of feelings churned. I was mortified. Embarrassed. Angry. Outwardly, I was silent. One of the stewards, however, was kind. He told me, "Wait. We still have many hours before we get to New York. I will find a way to tie this suitcase so that it can be carried safely." In the end, he had to tear out the cord from the headphone set to improvise the rope that adorned my suitcase. That's how I came to America. I'm sure you're wondering about the year. When do you think I arrived?

The year was 1984. Long before 9/11. Actually, thirty one years before 9/11, even in America, the land of equality, people sometimes judge you by the color of your skin.

1984 was an interesting year. Just the week before we arrived a man had shot 20 people dead in McDonald's restaurants in California. Later, I read the news that Indira Gandhi, India's prime minister was assassinated in Oct. by her own Sikh bodyguards. By then, I had also had my first brush with race.

I had applied for a graduate teaching assistantship (TA) at the University of Akron, Ohio, to teach Freshman English composition (undergraduate) as part of a teaching team. I had a Bachelor's degree in English Literature and a Master's degree in Library and Information Science. I was selected. I joined the team of 10 or so other TAs for the week long training. At the end of the week I was invited to the Dean's office and told the TA would not be awarded to me. It was very gently done, but the words summarizing the reason not to hire me as a TA have stayed with me. "How will it look if a person, who is not a native speaker of English teaches the language to our mid-western boys and girls?"

When the rest of my family and friends heard this, they were filled with anger on my behalf about "blatant discrimination" and "racism." I refused to accept it as such. Doing so made me feel ashamed of myself and who wants to be ashamed of themselves? Instead, I rationalized it. After all, this was my first semester in America. I had no experience of the American way. The Professor was right: I am a small woman and the undergraduates are big; I would not have been able to easily discipline or hold their attention. I didn't want to make waves. I wanted to fit in. I gave up the idea of earning a master's degree in English Literature. I moved into Education, where I felt I would not be as disadvantaged. That's precisely what I did for the next twenty years of my life. Every time I was perceived to be 'different' I focused on the positive and ignored the negative. I tried to fit in.

I could not hide the color of my skin or my heritage, but I could hide and nurture a rich inner life. Thus, on the surface I conformed. I completed my Ph.D. in Library and Information Science. I earned tenure, and became a professor in Santa Ana College/Santiago Canyon College, despite the harassment of colleagues. I can still remember the librarian at Santa Ana College who asked me: "You're from a third world country. How can you be so smart? How can you know so much about computers? Americans are supposed to be #1 in the world. We're the smartest. Is our government feeding us lies?"

Tired of the hostility which had begun to take a toll on my health (daily migraines and back problems), and uncaring of having won full tenure, I quit. UC Los Angeles snapped me up. Nevertheless, even here the professor who had hired me soon began to bully and abuse. "You're a post-doc, a dime a dozen," she warned. A Distinguished Professor and Presidential Chair at UCLA, after paying my salary at a rate that she set (I didn't negotiate), she reneged at the end of the semester. She authorized UCLA to reach back into my bank account and take back a large portion of the salary. Her excuse was that she had miscalculated. In the end I found I'd been paid at a rate of $10 an hour.

Fortunately, another professor from UC Santa Barbara hired me away with a fairer market rate salary ($75K per year). In the months that followed, Prof. Terence Smith also gave me the courage to become a full-time faculty, again, but this time at a Research I University. At the University of Arizona (UA), Tucson, I thrived for the first four years under the leadership of a supportive Dean. Soon, however, the negativity began. This time it was a new Director. She had been my classmate in the doctoral program at UIUC. I had even been instrumental in hiring her into UA. As usual, I did what I always do best. I run away from conflict. I planned to leave. In a few years I did.

I could never admit even to myself that racism and discrimination were a part of American academic life. So I squirreled these negativities away as inexplicable, nameless experiences. In the meantime, I also began learning about the categorization of race in American politics from my lived experiences with the US Census and job application forms that I was required to complete:

- In the 1980s, I, as a person from the Indian subcontinent was asked to check the box "white."
- By 2010, I became "Asian American"

The U.S. Census Bureau collects information on race following the guidance of the U.S. Office of Management and Budget's (OMB) 1997 Revisions to the Standards for the Classification of Federal Data on Race and Ethnicity. These federal standards mandate that race and Hispanic origin (ethnicity) are separate and distinct concepts, and that when collecting these data via self-identification, two different questions must be used.

In 2010, the race categories were as follows and the first five are generally considered the minimum on questionnaires:

- White
- Black or African American
- American Indian or Alaska Native
- Asian
- Native Hawaiian or Other Pacific Islander
- Some Other Race

The second question collected data on ethnicity: "Hispanic or Latino" and "Not Hispanic or Latino." The history of the Census categories can be seen in the figure that follows: What the Census call us: A Historical Timeline by the Pew Research Center.

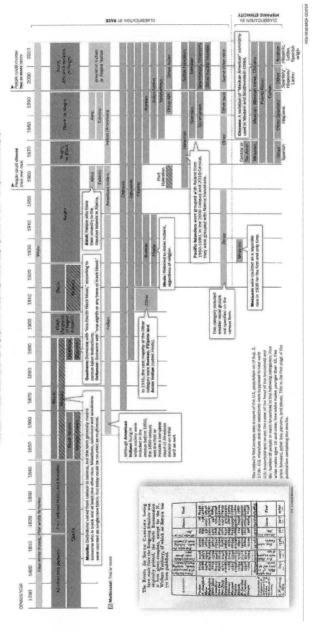

What Census Calls Us
A Historical Timeline

This graphic displays the different race, ethnicity and origin categories used in the U.S. decennial census, from the first one in 1790 to the latest count in 2010. The category names often changed from one decade to the next, in a reflection of current politics, science and public attitudes. For example, "colored" became "black," with "Negro" and "African American" added later. The term "Negro" will be dropped for the 2020 census. Through 1950, census-takers commonly determined the race of the people they counted. From 1960 on, Americans could choose their own race. Starting in 2000, Americans could include themselves in more than one race category. Before that, many multiracial people were counted in only one racial category.

42

For the 2020 census, some groups lobbied for a new race called MENA: Middle East and North African peoples. The Census Bureau, however, has decided against it for now. In 2020 the race categories will remain the same as they were in 2010. Ethnicity questions will be asked first, allowing collecting multiple Hispanic ethnicities such as Mexican and Puerto Rican, and explaining that specified race and ethnicity categories are socio-political constructs and should not be interpreted as being scientific or anthropological in nature.

By now, you should be fairly convinced too that race is not a real biological category. Race is a social category; in other words, race is socially and politically constructed. Scientists have been telling us this for years and my nameless experiences now have a name: Racialization.

As a dark-skinned woman from India, which does not have the social category of race, I found myself pigeon-holed in the land of freedom and equality. My key identifiers were: "minority," "woman of color," and "other." This is why racialization is also known as minoritization, coloring, and othering. My story also shows how people as well as issues are racialized, I found myself pigeonholed into the classic immigrant model and model minority stereotypes. For example, my success in the USA was ascribed not to the many socio-economic privileges I had enjoyed as a native of middle-class India but to America's level playing field. It was used to corroborate another myth about meritocracy: Anybody who works hard in America has an equal chance to succeed.

Racialization, minoritization, othering, coloring, all create a hierarchy of humanity. They are strategies for systematic oppression. They conflicted me. They violated me. When I try to make sense of my lived experiences, what I see are the five faces of oppression: violence, marginalization, exploitation, powerlessness, and cultural imperialism. I cannot claim to be the victim of physical violence but I can and will claim emotional oppression and resilience over structural racism which is still evolving and flourishing. How is this freedom for all?

43

Anita Coleman

Seeing Beyond Race

A memory haunts me. I am pregnant, carrying my first child, and I'm in hell. No, it wasn't depression during pregnancy. Nor was it the morning sickness, hell though it felt like! I was tormented by the thought that I was bringing a "dark-skinned" child into a world colonized by the idea that whiteness is synonymous with goodness. I was saddened by the thought of the painful repudiations and needless suffering this child would have to face.

As a young girl, growing up in India, I once overheard a conversation. "She is dark," said my aunt. "Not black like me," countered my mother. "Well, she's **mahniram**. But it would have been better if she were lighter skinned. Like her father," replied my aunt. **Mahniram** is a Tamil word which means having the complexion of a deer—dark brown.

Although the concept of race was unknown in India when I was growing up, dark children like me were perceived to be older, not as innocent, and less trustworthy. Colorism (color discrimination), I realized quickly, was sewn seamlessly into the fabric of Indian life. India's caste system, some believe, may derive from broad skin-color categories. Though the caste system was abolished in 1951, many years before I was born, it remained a social reality for many. My only brush with it was in the daily newspaper advertisements for

"fair and lovely" complexion creams and classifieds for
arranged marriages with "fair" brides.

In school, when I learned European and American
history, I struggled to reconcile the concept of race and its
constant companions of colonization, slavery, and privilege
with my born-again Christian faith. In college, the frequent
symbols and metaphors of English literature that equated
white with good and black with evil began to bother me. They
contradicted my biblical understanding that humankind is
made in the image of God. I saw beauty and goodness in all
people, including myself. My cinnamon-colored skin pleased
me, and the physical diversity among my family and friends
enchanted me. Skin that roamed the color spectrum of tertiary
grey to gleaming ebony, of composite browns to pale ivory
was a magical mystery that I admired.

Why then was I, a soon-to-be mother, now sad? I was
distressed because I knew the world didn't generally think like
I did. What kind of a home would the United States be for this
dark child? Would his life matter?

My child is now a grown man, and some of my fears
have come true. And so, as I begin to prepare for the last leg
of my own journey here on earth, I am compelled by
increasing racial tensions, my love for the United States, and
by my faith and hope in Jesus to write about race after decades
of silence. I have tried for years to convince myself
otherwise; however, in reality **there is nothing God-honoring
or even remotely life-giving about race.** Race is not a
biblical concept. Race is evil. The Bible reveals a God who
creates, affirms, and loves diversity, not race.

Race, as we know it, was constructed in modern Europe
by the unholy marriage of Christian theology with empire and
was driven by a need to justify economic domination. Today,
no two people will agree about the definition of race, but most
scholars are agreed that race is a socio-political category.
Race divides humans. Race does not unify our country. Why
then do faithful Christians continue to use racial categories to

describe people?

We do so for many reasons. One, we are deceived by the physical differences we see among people. Two, we are enslaved by powerful political forces, the media, and our culture. Race makes good drama and great news, and our country's economic strength was built on it! Finally, and most importantly, for the faithful, we also do so because many English translations of the Bible conflate or interpret the Greek words of *ethnos, laos, phylē*, and *genos* into the English word *race*. For an example, let's look at Revelation 7:9 (ESV):

> *After this I looked, and behold, a great multitude that no one could number, from every nation, from all tribes and peoples and languages, standing before the throne and before the Lamb, clothed in white robes, with palm branches in their hands...*

These words can be translated as follows, and, as you will see, there is no race!

> Nation = *ethnos*
> Tribe = *phylē*
> People = *laos*
> Language = *glossa*

What's more, biblical attempts to construct race are often foiled by God. In Genesis 11, God destroys the Tower of Babel because its creators wanted to "make a name for themselves," and establish their power as a singular, undiversified race of people. (One wonders who was going to be left out.) God confounds their attempt to reach into the heavenly realms by sowing seeds for linguistic diversity. New research has now shown that diverse languages and cultural expressions are critically beneficial to human growth, adaptation, and both individual and social development.

Yet, here we are, millennia later, still constructing race.

Since it first began in 1790, the US census categories have continued to change, reflecting our nation's confusion about race. (See the Figure, What the Census Calls Us: A Historical Timeline by the Pew Research Center).

From 1790 to 1840, the categories were: free white males, free white females, all other free persons, free colored males and females, slaves, and Indians (that is, Native Americans).

From 1850 to 1890 the census attempted to enumerate color categories such as Mulatto and Quadroon, a practice they soon abandoned. But it was only in 1870, in the first post-Civil War census, that the word *race* was used. The next 110 years, from 1900 to 2010, brought more changes:

> 1) 1930: "color races" introduced, and Mexicans counted for the first and only time as a separate race;
> 2) 1870: two new immigrant categories, Chinese and Japanese, added;
> 3) 1960: people choose their own race as census takers (enumerators) no longer assign race;
> 4) 2000: people choose two or more races, reflecting mixed ancestry;
> 5) 1970/1980: Hispanic is determined to be an ethnicity, not a race.

Changes proposed for the 2020 US Census included:

1) Eliminating the word *race;*
2) Eliminating "Negro" from the Black/African American category;
3) Adding a new category, Middle Eastern and North African (MENA).

Of the three changes only the second has passed and will appear in the 2020 Census. The US will continue to collect "race" data but there will be no MENA category. It is also worth noting here that the United Nations makes no recommendation for collecting data about race or ethnicity, and most countries don't collect race data. India, for example, eliminated the race category in 1951 (but not racism!).

The rationale in the US is that we need the racial data to create a more just society, especially for those historically oppressed and marginalized. However, racial discrimination and injustice have not disappeared. Despite our best attempts to build the beloved community with multi-culturalism, diversity, and pluralism, our language about race is neither biblical nor Christ-like. Insignificant visible differences of skin color and phenotypic variations are transformed into important identity labels, while innate human traits and spiritual gifts, such as faith, love, hope, and compassion, are neglected. We cannot dismantle racism while accepting and voicing its essential tenet: that we are divided into races.

The paradox is that to eliminate racism we must talk about race. Descriptors of color and hyphenated Americans, our human diversity—created, affirmed, and beloved by God—need a biblical vocabulary. We need labels that ground human identity not in the racial imagination and unjust hierarchies but in the ***imago dei*** (image of God) and the spirit of Jesus (Philippians 2:1–8).

We can begin to marvel at how wonderfully God has made people. One faithful starting point is to reflect on the words of Paul to the church in Rome: "Rejoice, Gentiles, with his people" (15:10). With acceptance and mutual respect, let us "welcome one another, just as Christ has welcomed you, for the glory of God" (15:7).

More radically, the church could stop using the categories assigned by the US Census. Racial categories are ultimately still all about power. As followers of Christ, we are not called to pursue power but to love. We can confess our addiction to power, our inability to love like Jesus, and stop racializing people. We can forge new behavior that represents, values, and celebrates our differences in biblical ways.

That won't happen as long as we insist on racial categories and who "counts" and who doesn't. Once, for instance, as a Presbyterian Women's member-at-large for Asian Americans, I was told: "You're from India. That's not Asian American." I apparently didn't count.

For one or more Sundays, we can give up our right to "our" way of worship by inviting a group with a different approach to worship to lead in their language and/or music. Activities and partnerships based on our mutual identity as Christians, and not on like-mindedness and racial similarities, will grow our acceptance and respect for others who are visibly different from us and strengthen our Christian witness. We will reclaim the power to promote healing, justice, and shalom (wholeness). For as Baldwin wrote, "If the word *integration* means anything, this is what it means: that we, with love, force our brothers to see themselves as they are, fleeing from reality and begin to change it."

Baldwin wrote this about his "white" brothers, but he also made it clear that "whiteness" is a mindset, prevailing then, as it is today, and held by people of all skin colors: "Color is not a human or personal reality; it is a political reality . . . and the value placed on the color of skin is always and everywhere and forever a delusion." *The Fire Next Time*.

The task of discovering new language for white, black, Indian, and other racial identity labels, and descriptors may well be impossible. Nevertheless, the church is called to this task and uniquely fitted to do so (I Peter 2: 9). I pray that we will do so.

Anita Coleman

Reclaiming Identity

Racialization meant that people sometimes saw me as white, black or other, depending on their own lived experiences, beliefs, and worldviews.

I remember a time, 1990, in San Diego, when a young French man, Patrice, asked me: "Why are they letting all these Asians into the country?" He was angry because the San Diego immigration authorities had just sent his girlfriend back to France. Apparently, she had come as a visitor the previous summer, taken up a job which she was not supposed to do, returned to France, and was trying to re-enter the country to keep the job. I looked at Patrice, puzzled. What did he think I was?

"Why are you telling me this, Patrice?"

"Because you're one of us. You understand," he said.

I was puzzled. What did Patrice mean? Who was "us"? When I asked, he replied, "Us. White people." That was my first insight into the construction of whiteness.

New immigrant groups are always on a journey to whiteness; the Irish for example weren't originally considered white.

Writers have teased out nuances of being black, white, and other in America. Ralph Ellison, for example, has written powerfully about invisibility. *"I am invisible. . . . It is sometimes advantageous to be unseen, although it is most often rather wearing on the nerves."* To Patrice the real me was invisible. The invisibility and complexity of racialization is best understood by another of my lived experiences, 25 years later, in 2015.

"Don't tell me, let me guess," he said. "Guess what?" I asked, puzzled by this stranger's remarks. I was at the gym, and my smile to him had been perfunctory. He was standing in front of the battle ropes with which I usually warmed up. "I'm learning how to recognize people's geographical origins," he answered. "You are very unusual looking. I bet I know where you're from."

"Go for it," I said, unrolling the ropes. "You're from Eritrea or Ethiopia," he responded. "We're all from Africa, aren't we?" I quipped, smiling. "I'm not far from there at all."

His face began to burn red. He blustered out an apology. Now, I felt sorry for him. Perhaps he was training to be an immigration officer and needed to be able to identify people's origins. After all, this was a question I've been asked all my life. Even when I was growing up in India, people would ask, "Where are you from?"

Given to dreaming, I would give a different answer every time: Sri Lanka, Madagascar, New Zealand. As I grew older, the diplomatic answer and what I hoped would invoke laughter became "Space cadet. Planet Earth." Few understood. Differentiation, I learned, was the crux of identity and group formation. Learning to see differences was the norm. Categorization was fundamental; without it, I was invisible. People required my geographic, social, economic, political, national, sexual, and religious labels in order to "see" me, in order for me to "compute."

America, the great melting pot, I thought, would be different. Coming to the United States, I wore a small gold cross on a chain around my neck proudly. The cross symbolized my identity in Christ, passionate devotion to God, and determination to live life the Jesus way. It had been possible in India, despite the fact that Christians were a minority. Might America be different? I still could recall my Dad saying, "At least you're going to a Christian country."

The concept of "an identity in Christ," however, proved to be almost unheard of in the Midwestern churches I frequented. The process of my racialization began. My markers included dusky skin, a "British" accent, graduate student status, and the diamonds in my ears. All these were commented upon quite candidly, but it was my adventurous confidence that puzzled the church people. They did not know what to do with me. Slowly church became irrelevant to my immigrant life. I left the church. The Spirit never departed from me, though, for I learned to embrace with bold joy any hyphenated American identity that onlookers saw fit to bestow on me: African, bi-racial, Islander, whatever! I was, after all, *imago Dei.*

I did well in school and work, with everybody praising my "WASP" (White Anglo-Saxon Protestant) work ethic. I landed jobs where I became living proof of the good things resulting from British colonialism and American immigration policy. In group photographs, my chocolate-brown color contrasted vividly with the pale white skin that surrounded me, a wonderful testament to American diversity. My "upper class" accent, petite figure, and "well-informed" intelligence—I have a Ph.D.—drew admiring remarks. Life in the ivory tower protected and indeed gave me many privileges. There I might have remained except life throws everybody curveballs. One day I caught mine, quit the academic life, and came back to the church, my core identity in Christ reinstated.

On the surface, in my new church, the old categories that made me a foreigner, a heathen, were gone. I taught women's Bible studies, was ordained a deacon, joined the missions committee, and served as coordinator for women's retreats. The trouble started when I began to exercise wider leadership. The church people were much more interested in celebrating my "different" heritage than in considering me one of their own. Since I'd grown up in a Christian home and had now spent more years in the United States than in India, this was not easy to do! I didn't speak an Indian language fluently, had worn Indian clothing only occasionally even while growing up in India, and there was no "back home." America was home. Still, I was obedient and since I loved to dress up, I learned to enjoy wearing Indian costumes, the fancier the better. I reconnected with friends in India, and began to do "mission" by speaking up on behalf of the poor there.

Soon I was oscillating between visibility and invisibility, between American and foreign cultures—often refusing positions of leadership, performing the submission a non-white woman ought to have (and it is a *performance*), always working hard, and being rarely listened to, heard, or invited into social life with native-born Americans.

Diversity, Hybridity. Fusion. Melting pot. We are all a mixed people. DNA studies are telling us that we're all migrated from Africa but came here to America in different ways. Obvious differences of skin color and phenotypical variations don't tell our whole stories. Global tribes are becoming more common as diasporas are created - Little Saigon, Little India, Little Italy.

Bias, categorization, and racism though are real. As I educated myself about race and its perniciousness, I began to seek a language that unifies us. What can that language be?

I'll give you a small example. I don't identify myself as "white," "black," or as a "person of color." Instead I embrace the language of my faith. I am a child of God. On census and other boxes I choose, Other – proudly. Labels that name us, even when we co-opt them, have the power to shame us. I don't want to give anybody that kind of power over me.

Growing up in a cosmopolitan city in India where there was no "white" dominant race, I was free to see and imagine myself in a way that I am sometimes not allowed to in the US. It took me a long time to take off the shackles people tried to put on me and reclaim myself as a child of God, woman, reader, writer, wife, mother, librarian, professor, researcher, faith leader, and more! I quit racializing myself. I began to use moral reasoning as a force of great good to draw people together. I began using the language of Christian anti-racism. Neither whiteness nor blackness nor the language of skin color, culture, and ethnicity describe our full humanity. The scholar West describes it below:

> In short, blackness is a political and ethical construct. Appeals to black authenticity ignore this fact; such appeals hide the political and ethical dimensions of blackness. That is why claims to racial authenticity trump political and ethical argument and why racial reasoning discourages moral reasoning. Every claim to racial authenticity presupposes elaborate conceptions of political and ethical relations of interests, individuals and communities. Racial reasoning hides these presuppositions behind a deceptive cloak of racial consensus, yet, racial reasoning is seductive because it invokes an undeniable history of racial abuse and racial struggle.

> … Where there is no vision, people perish. Where there is no framework of a moral reasoning the people close ranks in a war of all against all.
> (West, 1994).

References

Cornel West, p. 39-40, 48. chapter on The Pitfalls of Racial Reasoning in his book, Race Matters. First Vintage Books edition, 1994.

Anita Coleman

Caught in the Crossfire

Not black
Not white
Not quite
Not Hindu
Not Muslim
Not Indian
Not American.

Defined by what I'm not.
Desired for IQ IT.
Mistaken.

ABCD
Brownie
Colored
Dot-buster
Indo-nigger
Oreo
Sambo
Towel-head

Which tribe should I
choose?
Do I belong here?

We gon' be alright!

Oh, America! We, your
people
Vincent Chin
Trayvon Martin
Srinivas Kuchibotla
Baseball bat beaten
Gunshot at The Retreat
Murdered in Kansas.

Accidental. Activist. Anti-
racist
Chant. Coerce. Cajole.
No more incarceration
No more ravishing in the
Midwest
No burying genocide in
California
No re-segregating in the
East.

See me
Love me
Yearning to be
Human and free.

Anita Coleman

Aliens and Tenants, Our Citizenship is in Heaven

One planet. 57.3 million miles of surface land. 7.4 billion people. 59.5 million refugees and displaced peoples, of whom 51 percent are under the age of 18.

Sheikh Yassir Fazaga was once one of those refugees. Forced to flee his home in Eritrea at the age of 15, today, he is a well-respected Muslim leader and a mental health counselor at Access California Services. AccessCal is a non-sectarian organization that provides human services to local Arab and Muslim Americans, immigrants, and refugees. Speaking about the plight of refugees, he has said (I will paraphrase):

> Stories like mine are unusual. Many people in refugee camps are born there, and they die there. They become parents in the camp and grandparents too. The people who are able to leave the camps and re-integrate with mainstream society, often in a new country, as immigrants, asylum seekers, and citizens are far too few. To solve the refugee and other problems of the world *our concern must be global, and our influence, local*.

Fazaga's story and words resonate with my own beliefs about how faith, my identity as an American citizen, and allegiance to Jesus intersect.

In Leviticus, God's conversations with Moses reveal how God views humans: *With me, you are but aliens and tenants* (25:23). In the eyes of God, we are *all* aliens and tenants. God's lack of distinction between the aliens and citizens living on a land is also in keeping with the apostle Paul's pronouncement: *But our citizenship is in heaven* (Phil. 3:20).

When Christians align with God's view of our status on earth—as aliens and tenant citizens, whose true citizenship is in heaven—we will act and think as global citizens. Jesus died because he did not fall in line with the current ideas of Jewish and Roman nationalism. Following Jesus, we will explore how modern nation states and national citizenship(s) may be confining us in boxes with rigid boundaries that limit us spiritually and practically. Here are some fun ways, but by no means, all the ways, in which we can begin to explore our identity as global citizens:

1.   Make global connections personal.

I volunteer with a group in rural south India. They are the poorest of the poor, but they love the rural hills and the land in which they were born. They would prefer not to leave their families and villages, but their job opportunities are limited and the villages in which they live still shaped by centuries of cultural violence. I am slowly getting to know the challenges of sustainable Christian development in these far away remote areas; my childhood friend runs a rural community for peace and justice that provides vocational training there. Whom do you already know that you can join and support in developing countries—regularly, consistently, and relationally? Join them. Begin to listen to their stories.

2. **Go bananas!**

Really. Bananas are one of the most popular fruits in America (and worldwide). Our desire for cheap bananas, however, fosters an unfair supply chain that irreversibly damages farmers and their families in developing countries. Our consumer dollars, which can be a good thing, have a negative impact when we focus on buying things cheaply and ignore others' human rights. Try buying only those products that are vetted by groups and initiatives like the National Farm Worker Ministry and Fair Trade. Learn the truth about economic immigration and the devastating effects of human greed and unchecked capitalism.

3. **Start the journey to a free world by transforming American privilege into a kingdom asset.**

When our primary allegiance is to God, we will recognize and acknowledge that American citizenship confers enormous privileges. The US passport allows us to travel virtually anywhere in the world and to live in almost any country we choose. Refugees, the poor, and people in developing countries don't have these privileges or even the basic rights we take for granted such as access to education and jobs. Refugee camps are not places people were meant to live their entire lives. Seeing ourselves through God's eyes as universal aliens, we will begin to care for the human rights of all. We will want for them the same rich possibilities and freedoms of healthy human life. The European Union and ASEAN are examples of how nations that were once at war are now peacefully engaged in mutual trade, travel, and education across open borders. Get involved in the work of the United Nations Sustainable Development goals. If you haven't already done so, this journey can start with one small step of faith: Join the local chapter of your united nations association and commit to an annual event. Godspeed!

A MILLENIAL MALE:

FROM NATIONALISM AND MULTICULTURISM TO COSMOPOLITANISM

Ash Coleman, a second generation American, shares his identity development as a teenager. Moving from California where everybody knew him and his family, to Arizona, where nobody did, while still in high school, brought about a conflict. The move forced him to confront many of his own differences, visible physical markers, a blended and multi-cultural family who were highly educated and widely-traveled. God's grace helped him realize personal truths, that he is a beloved child of God and find his own resolution through research and reflection.

Ash Coleman

Lost in the Desert

The average American moves a lot and oftentimes the moves are painful. Research and statistics tell us that only about 30% of those who move don't find the changes painful. For the rest of us, the 70%, moving is a traumatic life event rated on par with divorce and death. Today, moving is an unavoidable trauma for millions. This is what I learned from my moving experience when I became lost in the desert.

In the summer after my freshman year of high school, my parents moved to the desert, specifically, Tucson, Arizona. We had been living in Irvine, California since I was in elementary school and I had just begun to enjoy high school. I had made the freshman basketball team and I was excelling in honors classes. We lived in America's safest city. My parents' jobs paid them decent salaries. It helped them own a nice house. We enjoyed the proverbial sunny skies of California by indulging in lots of activities outside the home.

In Irvine, I had achieved my dream of being an athlete when I made the basketball team. This had taken determination and years of practice. Moving to Tucson required me to try out a second time to make the high school basketball team. The Tucson climate and environment was so different that I did not even want to think of trying out again.

The hot sun quickly washed out my basketball athlete dream. Replacing that dream proved elusive. S weltering, barren Tucson made even dreaming a challenge.

Tucson is a part of the Sonoran Desert, a vast inhospitable region in the southwestern United States. It is considered to be a "place of paradoxes." Life forms that cannot exist anywhere else on earth, like the saguaro cacti and the Gila monsters, grow in abundance here. Desert rats, people who love the deserts, find beauty in this barren and diverse landscape. I saw only desiccated brown. Most notable is the unbearable scorching heat. The dry, intense desert heat changed me but not into a desert rat that could have handled it. Instead, I slowly became a night owl. I no longer skateboarded or played basketball but stayed up late nights to play video games obsessively. Irvine with its cool green landscapes haunted me. The dull, desert terrain where the saguaro cacti look like a gathering of drunken signposts, forced me into solitude. But before I could find myself, I became lost in the desert.

One particular instance is when I went with two buddies to a late night movie soon after 9/11. We were all under 17 and it was an "R" rated movie. The theatre had more than its usual share of noisy teenagers. Pretty soon we were all in trouble. City cops escorted us out of the theatre and into the security office. They questioned us separately.

We were accused of smoking pot. There was no evidence. Our parents had to come and pick us up. I could have sworn that we were innocent but I wonder now, did the cops pick on us because one of my friends, unnoticed by me, had been smoking? Or was it because we were all non-white? Did we just happen to fit their idea of teenage troublemakers? Perhaps we were just in the wrong place at the wrong time. Maybe it was a slow night for the cops who were bored in the desert as well.

My friends in Tucson were like me and yet, very different too. Like me, they spiked their hair and wore baggy clothes. Like me, some of them had parents who were immigrants from India. None of them though were in a visibly different family like me. Unlike me, they had cars. I envied their freedom, their ability to zoom around anywhere, the ease with which they spoke another language, and traveled the cultural distance between home and school.

For most of the year, I went to school and lived in Tucson with my Mom and stepfather, *Appa;* Appa is a Tamil word which means Father. I was the only child. Holidays were spent in San Jose, Northern California, with Dad, my biological father, step-mother, and half-brother. Here, I was the older sibling.

In Tucson, we spoke English, traveled widely during vacations, and ate foods from many lands. Mom and Appa had individual hobbies and loved solitude. No extended family lived with us. Neither Mom nor Appa had much interest in team sports. In this, they were unlike me; I had had aspirations of being a basketball player. I had made it to the freshman high school basketball team. The loss of that dream and the despair that followed was incomprehensible to them. I might even say that it was almost unnoticed.

In San Jose, my father, his family and their Indian friends spoke Tamil. Often, I had no clue what they were saying. Extended family, such as grandparents, was constantly visiting. The women wore saris and the men wore *lungis* or *dhotis*. Dad followed cricket matches, and read Indian newspapers. Spending time with his family was Dad's hobby, what he liked to do. We ate South Indian food: Dosa, chutney, rice and sambar. Dad was an enthusiastic American football fan, who never failed to celebrate Thanksgiving with the traditional turkey, and Thank God It's Friday evenings with pizza. Dad wanted me to work my way through college.

My biological parents had mixed cultures, in more ways than one.

I had been vaguely aware of my Indian-ness, for most of

my life, but in moving from California, which is culturally diverse and where people knew me, to Tucson, which is not as diverse and where nobody knew my parents or me, I became confused. I knew I looked Indian. I felt self-conscious and was always overly aware of myself. I wanted to be friendly with the American kids and dress like them, but since I was different it would be better to come off neutral. I became lost. I no longer knew who I really was or what I wanted anymore.

Ash Coleman

Roots and Wings

What does it mean to be a second-generation Indian American in the 21st century? For me, it means associating myself not only with American society and values but also partaking deeply of my Indian heritage and roots in Irvine, California. Intertwining these traditions is not as easy as it sounds but the result is a strong mix, a hybrid, blending the best of many cultures. Wait, did I really write many cultures? How many do I have? Is it possible for a person to have more than one culture?

My biological parents, lived the first part of their lives in India and came to the United States for professional graduate studies. Born and brought up as Christians, many western Judeo-Christian traditions were familiar, but they had to integrate new traditions related to food, drink, celebrations, values, and sports. Historical details about my parent's immigration to the United States, sociological details of the duality of Indian and American culture, and psychological details about identity have deepened my understanding of what it means to be a second-generation American. They also provided the context for a fuller understanding of my fundamental beliefs in equal rights and resources for humans *everywhere,* and irrespective of *any* differences. In other words, I see and treat people as individuals.

Historically, Indian immigration became common in the U.S. only after the passage of the 1965 Immigration and Nationality Act. This Act which liberalized immigration policies is responsible for the visible cultural diversity we see in the US today. The post-1965 immigrants largely from Asia, Latin America, and the Caribbean, were unlike earlier waves of immigrants who were mostly from Europe. This wave and their descendants transformed the U.S. from a largely bi-racial to a pluralistic society.

According to the 2000 census, Asian Indians in the U.S. numbered almost 1.7 million; they are among the wealthiest and most educated foreign-born groups, and were one of the fastest growing communities with a growth rate of 105.87 between 1990 and 2000. Indian Americans along with the other new immigrants did not fit neatly into the official categories for people in the US although by the 1990s Indian Americans were officially classed as "Asian Americans." Their racial and ethnic location in the US, however, as long been problematic and contested because they are dark-skinned. They are often mistaken for Hispanics or African Americans, confused with Native Americans and excluded from the Asian American umbrella, typically represented by China, Japan, Thailand, Korea, and Vietnam.

Immigration poses a threat to national identity. Large numbers of immigrants threaten a country's unity as they bring their own histories, traditions, customs, values, habits and ceremonies. Therefore, new immigrants often try to reconcile or submerge their ethnic identity with their American identity in order to successfully assimilate into the mainstream and in order to be perceived as patriotic Americans especially during times of hostility and war. The ethnic model which worked for European immigrants did not work as well for the large waves of post-1965 nonwhites. Racialization and minoritization made assimilation more difficult. The ethnic model also violates American values of individual identity and individual rights but racialization and selective acculturation, however, explain some aspects of my

Tucson experience. Selective acculturation is a process of identity formation and growth, whereby the second generation American incorporates into mainstream society while retaining some of the parent's culture and networks in order to be successful.

My Tucson experiences become easier to understand in the light of these details and the psychology that identity is formed during the teenage years. I was 16 years old when we moved to Tucson. In 16 years I had lived in at least 6 different places. Born in the rural mid-west I had been moved to and from coastal California two or three times as my Mom chased her American dream. I was the new kid over and over again and in all these new places I had to re-learn what the Indian background and my parents' blended families meant. For a few years, I'd found stability in Irvine where we'd lived since I was 9 years old. Moving to Tucson 6 years later, where once again, nobody knew my parents or me, I felt unable to cope with so much change and loss.

My research showed that other kids have had similar psychological problems with identity. John, a 16 year-old male with parents from multicultural backgrounds was referred to a psychologist because of his feelings of depression and lack of focus. John's trouble had started when his mother had been diagnosed with multiple myeloma. His psychological problems were rooted in his parents' multicultural background of Persia and East India. John's mother being diagnosed with an illness contributed to his feelings of depression, identity confusion, and social anxiety. John was struggling with his identity as he was only 16, and it was still being formed.

I, as a second-generation Indian American in a blended family, faced lots of choices about food, dress, and hobbies and other aspects of the visible identity and invisible self. Growing up in Irvine, which is known for its diversity, I noticed that most of my friends tended to have families that speak the same language (English), dress alike (jeans and t-shirts), eat the same food on major national holidays (turkey), and enjoy team sports (baseball, basketball, football, etc.). My experiences were different.

After all, I've travelled a lot more than the average American. Often, Mom remembers the time she and Dad took me to India when I was 10 months old. Dad reminisces about the times he's taken me there, when I was in the 5th grade, a quiet 8-year old, and again, when I was a cheery, middle school 7th grader. *Appa* reminds me of an idyllic summer visit to Evanston where he was born and grew up and then down to the county of the Dred-Scott decision where I was born.

Then, there are my high school summers. Every year, with my mom, I traveled to different places: Norway, Sweden, Denmark, England, Spain, and Finland. One long night we cruised through the world's most beautiful archipelago lying atop Europe. As far as the eye could see there was life-giving water and ethereally lighted skies. The chain of islands lying like brilliant, scintillating emeralds reminded me of my many successful moves and changes, success over challenges.

Like my parents, I too want the American dream, a job I love, decent pay and standard of living, and a nice home. Unlike them, I've heard about global warming all my life and what we, trend-setting materialistic over-achieving Americans and world leaders, are doing to our planet. Unlike them, I don't need to search for a place that feels like home in a strange new country. Unlike them, I must grow my wings and roots at the same time.

With roots from ancient India, my birth in the American heartland, and growth in faith, I deeper for my values and saturate myself more firmly into the American fabric.

With my wings, from the innovative Golden State of California, forged by the childhood I remember best, as well as our many moves and world travel, I fly high to become a part of the shrinking, global world. I am secure about my place and my life in the land where I was born. I watch the Eucalyptus trees on Irvine Blvd. and wonder if they are growing taller or if it is all my imagination. I can monitor the Great Park as it is built up new and watch it grow old, needing refurbishing. Whenever I see brown I can remember my move to the desert and be glad that the saguaro cacti, in the end, helped me find the right way home.

I am a man of God. A man of God doesn't hurry. A man of God doesn't worry. A man of God thrives wherever he is.

Although I began writing in order to understand myself, as I continued to write, I discovered that everybody needs wings and roots. "Unity in diversity," sounds trite but it is true; it is a philosophy and phrase, often used to describe India from ancient times, and more recently, Europe, South Africa, and the U.S. A. because of the multi-ethnic, multi-religious, and multi-lingual peoples and pluralistic societies.

My parents transformed themselves by making choices about the culture they would keep, adopt, and adapt. They developed cosmopolitan ways of living and hybrid forms of identity. My mom bakes to relax. She tries to live like the natives when we travel, with some hilarious and frustrating results! Dad loves being a family man. Appa is a creative, out of the box thinker. My parents' choices are reflected in my own preferences. My favorite food is the Mexican taco. I like to keep things simple. I have been empowered by my parents and the values of a pluralist 21st century U.S. to accept myself as created and loved by God, and unashamedly claim myself as American too.

Teenage years, high school, individual and social identity, and moving are all common human experiences. They've led me to think more deeply about myself and increased my awareness of the fundamental humanity of all people, no matter the different heritages and backgrounds. To live the new American dream – doing a job you love while living a life of freedom and luxury that is not available to the majority of the world – you must grow wings and roots that acknowledge, embrace, and celebrate the richness of human cultures around and within us. After all, we're all from Africa ultimately.

The presumption that each individual ultimately has a single, well-defined culture is false. In fact, we all experience a plurality of cultures. And as became evident to me, as humans, we are all a combination of cultures that can vary depending on the context.

RISE, SHINE, BE WOKE

FROM THE BELOVED COMMUNITY TO THE POOR PEOPLE'S CAMPAIGN: TRANSFORMATIVE INTEGRATIVE ANTI-RACISM

Stories and essays by Anita Coleman about transformative, integrative, everyday anti-racism in action. When we submit to God, the Holy Spirit leads us gently into practices that contribute to anti-racism: Advocacy, Activism, Active Listening, Acknowledging and Examining Privilege, Cultural Humility, Faithful Rhetoric (voice), Lifelong Learning, Racial Equity, Racial Healing, Reflection (Contemplation, Meditation), Research, Resilience, Sharing Power, Simple Living, Solidarity, Story-Telling and Truth-Telling, Witnessing, and more.

The Tapestry:
My Anti-Racism Story

My eyes opened to another perfect California day. The usual cool, foggy marine layer that coastal California tends to get in June was missing but my day soon turned cloudy anyway. That was the morning, Thursday June 18, 2015 many of us in the United States woke up to the news of a shooting the previous evening at the Emanuel AME church in Charleston, South Carolina. Nine people were killed because a stranger, who said he was a Christian, had been welcomed into their Bible study. He had returned death for the love he received.

I became frustrated when friends, some from the same Christian faith as the killer claimed to be, couldn't empathize. They rationalized: "He was just a crazy person, Anita, not racist. The African American church did the right thing to forgive him so quickly."

The inability to empathize triggered my intellectual curiosity. These were good people who loved and followed Jesus. Where was Christian belief in action negating, invalidating, and transforming racist systems?

I searched library catalogs, electronic databases in academic disciplines, news, and other popular information resources on the web. In the *Library of Congress Subject Headings* (*LCSH*), I found answers. There was only one subject heading for Anti-racism but hundreds of sub-headings for Race, Race discrimination, Race relations, Racism, and more. Similarly, most people I spoke to did not know what anti-racism meant. They equated it with color-blindness and often said: "I don't see race. I treat all people alike."

I began to study, teach, talk about anti-racism, and to develop the Anti-racism Digital Library and Thesaurus, an open access clearinghouse for online materials about anti-racism and related ideas.

It is fast becoming a tapestry that traces and connects my inter-lacings with people locally, regionally, and globally. I am slowly becoming engaged in anti-racism education and striving to see with Christ's eyes, adopt life with a new language, and build relationships that shape a fair society for all people created "imago dei" (in God's image): The Beloved Community. God's kin-dom.

It began simply, by me using my professional expertise to curate visions and experiences, tools and a vocabulary for anti-racism: The Anti-racism Digital Library. On June 17, 2016, one year after the shooting, I presented my paper on **"Theology, Race and Libraries***"* at the Annual Conference of the American Theological Librarians Association, Long Beach and described the communities behind the Anti-racism Digital Library. Two years after the shooting, on June 17, 2017, I presented another paper, **"Using the Anti-racism Digital Library and Thesaurus to Understand Information Access, Authority, Value and Privilege,"** again, at the Annual Conference of the American Theological Librarians Association. This time the conference was in Atlanta, Georgia, once the home of the African American scholar W.E.B. DuBois. In my paper I discussed how antiracism information literacy can be taught and learned as part of theological and religious studies education. I explained how anti-racism scholarship has become an integral part of my own spiritual formation and professional development too.

Racism is not just about individual bias or prejudice. Racism is a failure to grasp the essential nature of the Trinity –

God in community, hoarding nothing, sharing power and resources, serving all. Anti-racism is the Spirit's remedy, tandem knitting us, transcending nativism, tribalism, the fears that skin color, facial features, and other differences, such as non-whiteness, invoke. Anti-racism is about co-creating God's kin-dom. The extravagant, enigmatic tapestry continues to teaches me that an identity in Christ is an anti-racist one: Seeing and loving God in everyone means freedom and fairness for all. It means choosing a simple life, doing a few small things, as Mother Teresa was fond of saying, with great love.

"I want you woven into a tapestry of love, in touch with everything there is to know of God. Then you will have minds confident and at rest, focused on Christ, God's great mystery." Colossians 2: 2 (The Message)

When the homelessness crisis came home to my city this Spring 2018, on the third anniversary of Charleston AME shooting, my anti-racist voice and identity was Spirit-led into advocacy and activism. Affluent homeowners, many of whom are new immigrants, stereotyped, stigmatized, and protested successfully against the siting of housing for the poor homeless in our city. Appalled by the language I heard used to describe the poor during the public comments at City Council meetings and on social media, I wanted to change the narrative by bringing a different voice and de-mystifying homelessness. That's how it started.

The two top factors driving homelessness are economic insecurity and housing shortages. I wrote Op Ed blogs, went to meetings, and met lots of people. I launched a campaign, Irvine for Everyone Sign On Sheet, to help end homelessness in my county. Within a few days, hundreds or residents signed it. I took a small group to meet the Mayor. He responded to our advocacy and he even encouraged me to keep up the public education campaign. The suburbs, it turns out are facing classism (nimbyism) and the field is ripe for the faith-filled rhetoric of anti-racism. What an amazing tapestry.

From the Racial Imagination of Categorization, Bias, and Prejudice to the Christian Imagination of the Imago Dei and God's kin-dom

I want to suggest two important points at the outset:

1) The Bible does not affirm race. Rather, Scripture reveals a God who created humans *imago dei,* and loves diversity.

2) There is now a version of the prayer Jesus taught his disciples in which the word 'kin-dom' is substituted for kingdom. Kin-dom is more in keeping than kingdom with the non-violence of Jesus.

The tendency to put people into "racial" and other boxes comes from the innate human skill for creating categories. Categorization is central to what makes us human but most of it is automatic, unconscious; we become aware of it, only in problematic cases. Race, a category constructed by humans, is now a huge problem. It is based on the classical view of categories which is ~2000 years of human thinking in a very particular way. I've simplified it as follows:

1) **Categories are based on reason:** Categories have clear boundaries and share properties. Things and people (and whatever else we're organizing) are

logically categorized together on the basis of what they have in common.

2) **Categories are hierarchical:** There is specific order, arrangement, gradation, above/below/same levels.

3) **Categories are natural**: As we move around the world we categorize both man-made and natural things. We come to believe that the categories of our mind naturally fit the things that are there in the world (that is, what we see is what we categorize). Most of our categories, however, are not of things, they are of abstract entities. Social relationships, events, actions, emotions, illnesses, governments, entities in science and folk theories like electrons and colds are all things we make up, create, construct, and build.

The classical view about categories is the dominant, Western, still predominant view today even though recent research of ~80 years shows otherwise. The new research is from many different disciplines, has been conducted with diverse people groups around the world. It has many names: Cognitive Models; Prototype-based categories defined by cognitive models; Prototype Theory. These theories offer a different and new view about categories. The main points are

1) **Human categorization is not solely based on reason.** Human emotion, intuition, even imagination play a far larger part in the making of categories. In a fascinating article, *What, If Anything, Is a Zebra?* (Gould, 1983) discusses how scientists, a group that you would expect to be logical, specifically, different taxonomist groups differed on categories.

2) **Many cultures do not categorize hierarchically.** In other words, there are many categories that don't have above/below levels. Some are level (rounds).

3) **No universal conceptual system has been found; this means categories are humanly-made**. The environment, lived experiences, imagination, antipathies, bias, and prejudices play roles, often conscious, sometimes unconscious (implicit).

The modern racial imagination is the result of human categorization and susceptible to bias and prejudice. Very simply, race is a social construct of the Western racial imagination forged by the marriage of philosophy and theology driven by the Enlightenment's need for "capital."

What is the Christian imagination? Here's what I suggest.

Genesis 1: 26a Then God said, "Let us make humankind in our image, according to our likeness…" This is the *imago dei* (not necessarily like God physically but in attributes such as intelligence, imagination, creativity, emotion, and more).

Revelation 7: 9 is often quoted in support of racial justice; but the Greek word translated here as *race* according to *Strong's Concordance* (#1884) is not race. Rather it is *ethnicity*.
Éthnos (from *ethō*, "forming a custom, culture") – properly, people joined by practicing similar customs or common culture; nation(s), usually referring to unbelieving Gentiles (non-Jews).
God is not affirming race a socially constructed concept but a naturally occurring diversity of cultures, languages, and people groups.

Matthew 6: 10 is one of the verses in the prayer that Jesus taught his disciples. Mujerista Liberation theology substitutes the word kin-dom for kingdom:

"Your kin-dom come,
Your will be done on earth,
as it is in heaven."

Kin-dom reflects Jesus' radical vision of God's reign more accurately. Jesus created his new family of disciples and followers based on love. In God's kin-dom a person's life and liberation cannot be at the expense of another. Relationships cannot be authoritative or exploitative. Such kinship that offers a family of inclusion, justice, and restoration of faith and society is an intrinsic part of the Christian imagination.

How I Turned My Body Into a Canvas for Solidarity

My body can be the canvas for messages of solidarity.

In the wake of increasing intolerance in 2015, the Newport-Mesa-Irvine Interfaith Alliance of which my church, St. Mark Presbyterian, is a member (I serve on the board), my pastor, other faith leaders, and over 200 supporters showed up at the local Islamic mosque one Friday during Advent. The following Friday we visited a local Sikh Gurdwara and after worship shared in the *langar* (vegetarian meal). I wanted to do more, and I wanted something that everyone could join. Besides prayer and parley, presence and purse, how else could we express solidarity? The surprising answer came in a series of diverse verses from Scripture:

> "Strength and honor are her clothing and she is confident of the time to come." (Prov. 31:25 CEB)

> "For while bodily training is of some value, godliness is of value in every way, as it holds promise for the present life and also for the life to come." (1 Tim. 4:8 ESV)

> "Or do you not know that your body is a temple of the Holy Spirit within you, whom you have from God? You are not your own, for you were bought with a price. So glorify God in your body." (1 Cor. 6: 19–20 ESV)

"Then God said, 'Let us make man in our image, after our likeness." (Gen. 1:26a CEB)

"The Word became flesh and made his home among us. We have seen his glory, glory like that of a father's only son, full of grace and truth." (John 1:14 CEB)

"In him, we have obtained an inheritance, having been predestined, according to the purpose of him who works all things according to the counsel of his will, so that we who are the first to hope in Christ might be to the praise of his glory." (Eph. 1:11–12 ESV)

A tentative plan coalesced into action when I received a head-wrap as a surprise Christmas gift. Impetuously, courageously a young college student Bailey and I consecrated Epiphany Sunday; Bailey wore an Indian sari (from my tradition), and I put on the head wrap (from her tradition) for worship. Later, we took pictures and posted them on Facebook with the hashtags: #NotCulturalAppropriation #TheWorldIsMyOyster #SolidarityWithHumanity. If you, like me, are looking for simple solidarity with a huge impact, I invite you to try out this fun little fashion game.

Practice Anti-racism

Team up with someone from a different cultural heritage than your own; each of you should choose an authentic costume or piece of clothing from the other's heritage (e.g. for men, Pakistani stole, *sherwani* or *kurta*; for women, the Indian sari, African headwrap).

Learn about the clothing. Make a commitment to wear it to church and one other public place (work, school, grocery).

Wear it once a month or bi-monthly. When you wear it, engage someone in conversation about it. Ask the other person about the traditions and meaning of the clothing.

Share your experiences about wearing it with one another. Take pictures and post them on social media. If you post it on social media, come up with catchy tags: Examples: #FashionistasActivistas #SolidarityWithHumanity #APraiseForHisGlory #WeAreAllFromAfrica.

The point here is not simply the clothing. The world's not going to change by holding up a sign for a photo, donning a hoodie on social media, or wearing a hijab for a day. If done in isolation, this risks not only cultural appropriation but also smug self-satisfaction.

The point is what this kind of clothing leads to. When done in partnership with another person, this reciprocity of clothing leads to an interchange of ideas and experiences. We get to know somebody different on a more personal level. It invites others to join in by making it public. Solidarity and interconnectedness become tangible. After all you didn't just toss anything on that you thought "represented" another culture; rather, you submitted to the leading of another person from that culture and you trusted them to help you look good. And that kind of public, power-shifting, interdependence *could* very well change the world.

Prayer: God of grace and hope, I'm tired of the rhetoric of intolerance, hate, and selfishness. Globalization, climate change, and terrorism among other things are making us one small world with too many divisions, but you made us one humankind long before! Clothe me in strength and honor, God of beauty and unity. Train me in godliness, Holy One. Open my eyes so I see the "other" as your child, created in God's image. Increase the time I spend in the company of others who are not like me, just as Jesus did when he came and lived among us. May I use my body as the canvas to show solidarity with all humankind. May I be a praise for your glory, and above all, may your kingdom come quickly. All this I ask in the name of Jesus. Amen.

What is Anti-racism?

"Desegregation is only a partial, though necessary, step toward the ultimate goal that we seek to realize. Desegregation will break down legal barriers, and bring men together physically. But something must happen so as to touch the hearts and souls of men so that they will come together, not because the law says it, but because it is natural and right... . [The goal] is reconciliation and the creation of the **beloved community**." - Rev. Dr. Martin Luther King, Jr.

In 1954 the Civil Rights struggle gained momentum when the Supreme Court made segregation illegal in public schools in the case of Brown v. Board of Education. Then, in 1957, President Eisenhower signed the Civil Rights Act of 1957 into law. This was the first major civil rights legislation since Reconstruction and it allowed federal prosecution of anyone who tried to prevent someone from voting. It also created the first commission to investigate voter fraud. Another of the most famous moments of the Civil Rights Movement was the March on Washington in August 1963. More than 200,000 Americans congregated peacefully in Washington D.C. Rev. Dr. King, Jr. gave his famous *I have a dream* speech which became synonymous with freedom and equality. The following year, the Civil Rights Act of 1964 was signed into law in July. A year later, the Voting Rights Act of 1965 was passed and then, in 1968, the Fair Housing Act.

The Civil Rights period was an empowering time for

African Americans. They made significant legal gains but King wanted more for all people. In May 1967, a year before he was killed, King announced that the Civil Rights era was becoming the era of Human Rights. He and other civil rights leaders were going to launch a Poor People's Campaign against the triple evils of poverty, racism, and militarism (violence). "I choose to identify with the underprivileged. I choose to identify with the poor. I choose to give my life for the hungry. I choose to give my life for those who have been left out … This is the way I'm going." King said.

The first Poor People's Campaign launched in 1968 had limited impact (King and Kennedy had been assassinated). Exactly fifty years later and two years in the making, there's a revival Poor People's Campaign. Under the leadership of the Rev. Dr. William J. Barber, II and the Rev. Liz Theoharis **A National Call for Moral Revival** and **A Moral Agenda Based on Fundamental Rights** has been issued, and a **Forty Days** resistance started May 13 and culminated in a Global Solidarity Day on June 23. The campaign is protesting against a huge number of issues ranging from systemic racism, voting rights frauds, rising inequality, poverty, housing and food insecurity, incarceration, and ecological devastation to islamophobia, mis-treatment of indigenous people and other vulnerable populations. If you haven't yet become familiar with the 2018 Poor People Campaign, I encourage you to do so. They have created *We Rise: A Movement Songbook* and are using music, art, and culture to build confidence, courage in challenging situations and set the stage for transformation. They are also training people in non-violent resistance, anti-racism strategy successfully used during the Civil Rights.

Americans have been divided along racial and partisan lines for a long time. Discussing race theoretically, presenting statistics about racism, or sharing how racialization affects different groups of people is helpful. But it is not going to stop or mitigate the evils or bring about racial equity. We have a better shot at dismantling racism and achieving justice when we link our talks to calls to action and encourage the practice of transformative integrative anti-racism as spiritual formation that keeps changing us, people in our sphere of influence, institutions, and systems. That's what I've tried to show in this book:

- Sharing the lived experiences of people, you may know, I hope, will increase understanding of the connection between faith and anti-racism;
- Provide sacred spaces to discover, shape, and grow by reflecting on our own lived experiences, original purpose and place in unique, historical context;
- Follow the Spirit's calling to restore people and bring racial healing, equity, and justice in our sphere of influence, social networks, and corner of the world

Anti-racism calls people of all skin colors to a negative task. Those of European American origin are asked to critique white skin privilege by acting against their own self-interest. Which rational person wants to give up the things that make life very comfortable? Life is hard enough as it is. It is very difficult to persuade anybody to join a cause which appears on the surface to be against their own interests. Whiteness, like blackness and color, is also not a monolith. Having white skin privilege doesn't mean that one may not face discrimination of other kinds such as able-ism, age-ism, class-ism, gender-ism, or sex-ism. The lived experiences of people in this book we find that diversities exist within all of the color constructions – white, black, other. We also see that there is not one identity, but different identities that intersect. People are complex, identities are fluid, and our journeys and lived experiences are varied. When this is ignored, all forms of racism continue.

The good news is that Christian faith builds affirmative anti-racist identities for all people, irrespective of color and a racialized past. When we use spiritual formation as the lens for identity, we will find ourselves questioning the systemic causes of oppression, exploitation, violence, uncovering how we may be contributing to it, and moving towards the beloved community and reconciliation. Being honest before God will bring us face to face with our prejudices, help us acknowledge privilege, and divest from it when oppression is also present. This is transformative, integrative anti-racism.

BOOK STUDY GUIDE

Week 1: LEADING EDGE BABY BOOMERS: FROM SEGREGATION TO COMMUNITY

Leading edge baby boomers are people born between the years of 1945 and 1954. The defining point is that they came of age during the Vietnam War. They also experienced widespread rising prosperity, the end of segregated public facilities, and the triumph of the Civil Rights movement. Politically, the Baby Boomer years (born 1945 – 1964) were dominated by the New Deal Coalition forged by Franklin D. Roosevelt, of diverse groups of people: Democratic state party organizations, trade unions, racial, ethnic, religious groups, poor people who worked together. **Community, Diversity, are some of the anti-racism beliefs/values and Racial Equity, an anti-racism goal that can be discussed in this section.** Look up the definitions of these terms in the glossary and use them as you discuss the questions below.

1) Susan challenges the notion of meritocracy. What do you think? Do you have a similar or dis-similar story to share?

2) In your life, where do you experience the most diversity today (e.g. church) and where do you find it the least?

3) How did 6-year old Marvella experience community? What can we learn and practice from this?

4) What are the many influences that shaped Francena's life?

5) Sharon: "That I could do my little bit, in an everyday way, to help someone, somewhere, made a difference to me." What are some of the everyday ways in which you practice anti-racism?

6) Sharon also writes: "I have never been one who needs roles models to look like me." Discuss.

Week 2: A BABY BUSTER: FROM INTEGRATION TO INCLUSION

Baby busters, also known as Generation X, the 13th Generation ever to be called Americans are people born between 1965 to 1980; some scholars prefer 1961-1981. Busters are so called because there was a significant decrease in the birthrate , i.e. population. They were born a decade or more after the 1954 historic ruling of Brown v. Board of Education which desegregated public schools. Approximately, 50% of baby busters come from single-parent households. Their biggest technological influence was the personal computer which had become common in schools in 1980s. Busters created the online networks and tools that powered the entrepreneurial, technological, economy engine of the 1990s. This generation also learned from watching the failures of the Baby Boomers. **Learning/ Education, Safe Spaces, Worship,** and **Hospitality** are beliefs, activities, values that energize Stephanie. Explore these terms from the glossary.

1) Name specific phrases and sentences in Stephanie's writings and your own corresponding feeling (s).
2) What are some of the differences in the Christianity that is practiced by the enslaved versus the masters?
3) Knowledge is one of Stephanie's tools for empowerment as are her Great Grandmother's teachings. Are these safe spaces? Who and what are your safe spaces? What kind of safe spaces do you create and use for developing your anti-racist identity?
4) Stephanie writes that "personal development, self-reliance, and reciprocity" as well as the Golden Rule and discipline are important to her. Discuss these and other spiritual disciplines and practices from her essay.
5) What are the elements that make up Stephanie moral code? Do you have a similar moral code? How does it help you?
6) Reflect on the picture of the damaged bus in the essay "I was right." What feelings and thoughts does it bring up? Try to put yourself in Stephanie's shoes and imagine that day.

Week 3: A LEGAL ALIEN: FROM IMMIGRATION TO CITIZENSHIP

Anita Coleman writes about her lived experiences as a first generation immigrant, from growing up without race in India, to experiencing racialization, and cultivating an identity in Jesus Christ. Use **Race, Racism, Racialization**, and related terms along with **bias** and **white supremacy** in the glossary to discuss this section. .

1) What are some of the ways Anita seeks to be accepted?
2) How has the geography of Anita's birth affected her life?
3) Does Anita's definition of heavenly citizenship resonate with you? Is it useful for anti-racism?
4) Compare Anita's stories with that of another first generation immigrant.(or born-American) whom you know. What are some of the similarities and differences?
5) Writing her stories helps Anita acknowledge her sadness and releases her from shame. Is this a form truth-telling? What are the elements of witnessing, resilience, and reconciliation in her stories?

Week 4: A MILLENIAL MALE: FROM NATIONALISM AND MULTICULTURISM TO COSMOPOLITANISM

Ash Coleman, a second generation American, shares his teenage identity development. **Resilience, Cosmopolitanism** and **Culture** (and all it variants), come alive in Ash's stories. Explore them along with **Bias**, **Ethnicity**, **Exceptionalism,** and **White Supremacy** in the glossary.

1) Psychology shows that human identity is based on two things: occupation (what the person does for a living) and ideology (fundamental beliefs). How do Ash's stories fit or not fit this kind of identity formation paradigm?
2) How close or distant do you feel to Ash? Is his background similar or unlike yours? What did you learn?
3) Discuss the American Dream. Has it changed?

Weeks 5 and 6: FROM THE BELOVED COMMUNITY TO THE POOR PEOPLE'S CAMPAIGN:

Allyship, Solidarity, and Witness-Bearing (Christianity) are everyday actions that build God's kin-dom and bring racial justice and equity to our society.

1) What is your anti-racism story? Perhaps you have an anti-racism image, poem or song? Write it. Draw it. Sing it. Craft it. Share it. Meditate on it. Enjoy it.
2) What are your memories and impressions of the Civil Rights movement? The Vietnam War? The 1968 Poor People's Campaign? The 2018 Poor People's Campaign? Other current events (e.g. Black Lives Matter)?
3) By reading the lived experiences of others we can see that we share a collective past that tenuously connects us to a present that we struggle to understand. Do you agree or not? Discuss. What are some of the historical other connections you feel?
4) What have you learned about the Anti-racism Digital Library? How do you plan to contribute or use it?

WEEK 7: Comparative Discussions (Optional: You could also start with these overall questions of the whole book)

1) Compare the stories as you read them. To whom do you feel closest? Most distant? In attitude? Belief? Culture? Age? What else?
2) What have you learned about oppression and oppressors in these stories?
3) What is the role of faith? When you think of Presbyterian Women or your church family do they come alive to you as 'sisters of the faith' or God's 'kin-dom'? Discuss.
4) Faith, family and education play key roles in the narratives. How have faith, family, and education shaped you?
5) What is one strong message (something that inspires or motivates you) in each story and/or essay?

ACTIVITIES

Bias Activity: Scientific studies show that we make snap judgments about another person based on their appearance in less than 100 milliseconds. Imagine that neither the word *race* nor the concept exists. List the words that come to your mind when you think of yourself, neighbor, a friend, a member of your family, a stranger seen recently. In what circumstances is it important to describe a person's physical characteristics? Share and discuss the descriptions. What did you think of the way your neighbor described you? Did you feel racialized or not? Did you use skin color labels in the descriptions of yourself, your neighbor? Why or why not? How can we describe others without using skin color labels?

Glossary – Group Activity: Each person selects a Glossary term. Go around the group and have each person read the definition . Listen and make a note of terms that **attract you** or make you feel **uncomfortable.** At the end of each term and definition reading share and discuss as honestly as possible.

Images Activity: Examine the picture of Francena's house and read her memoir. What does it reveal about the American Dream of home ownership?

Internet/WWW based Activity: Go to the Anti-racism Digital Library (http://endracism.info). Download the **Growing a Personal Anti-racist Voice and Identity**. Do the study on your own or in a small group.

"Lived Experience" Activity: Interview a person who has lived through an important event in history (e.g. Executive Order 9066, or any of the watershed moments of the Civil Rights movement such as MLK, Kr.'s I have a dream speech). What did you learn that cannot be found or is different from the historical record?

The Anti-racism Digital Library
http://endracism.info/

"Libraries are always inclusive, never exclusive," so said Cynthia Hurd, a 31-year library employee who died in the Emanuel AME church shooting in June 2015. The Anti-racism Digital Library is dedicated to all 9 victims of the AME Church Charleston shooting: Rev. Sharonda Coleman-Singleton, Cynthia Hurd, Rev. Clementa Pinckney, Rev. Daniel Simmons Sr., Myra Thompson, Tywanza Sanders, Rev. DePayne Middleton-Doctor, Susie Jackson, Ethel Lance.

The Anti-racism Digital Library is my research and development initiative that serves as a clearinghouse for information resources on anti-racism. The resources are organized into collections such as **Presbyterian Women and The Intercultural Church.** The goal of the library is to offer new language for fueling the human imagination with concepts and categories that describe essential humanity. The collections bring together information resources created by diverse people, groups and projects that are adapting anti-racism and building inclusive and caring communities. There is a glossary which will help ultimately to develop a Thesaurus for the indexing and cataloging of information resources about anti-racism.

Anti-racism is defined as some form of focused and sustained action, by a mix of people which includes inter-cultural, inter-faith, multi-lingual and inter-abled communities with the intent to change a system or an institutional policy, practice, or procedure which has racist effects. Intersectional invisibility, that is, discrimination and oppression in the margins and intersections of society based on categories of class (social, economic, education), gender, language, and race/ethnicity, culture, faith, making the global local, empowering and supporting individuals and groups to act locally while interacting and collaborating regionally, nationally and internationally to eradicate systemic injustice, and enable equity and justice, are of special interest and the foci of the library collection development efforts.

As an object of sociological research there has been little scholarly attention paid to the study of "anti-racism." Themes related to "race," "racism," "discrimination" and "ethnicity" tend to make up the bulk of the literature. Bibliographic evidence, from library catalogs as well as knowledge structures, such as the schemes of organization and control that are used to describe information resources, confirmed this, in the fall of 2015. A subject search for "anti-racism" in the King Library catalog of San Jose State University and San Jose City retrieved 15 resources while a subject search for "racism," on the other hand, retrieved 2,037 resources. A subject search for "anti-racism" in the Library of Congress catalog retrieved 108 resources and 5,349 resources about "racism." Google had a similar rate of return: "anti-racism" had 12, 400,000 hits while "racism" had 70, 200,000 hits.

The research investigated the treatment of the *Library of Congress Subject Heading* "anti-racism" in order to understand its strengths and limitations.

The tenets of Critical Race Theory hold that race is a social construction, racism is endemic and institutional. Newer theories of categorization suggest that human categorization does not conform to the classical views of hierarchies and clear boundaries, and that language plays a powerful role in how we construct categories. How can we eliminate racism if we keep using the language of race and don't understand that of anti-racism?

Thus, my research also looked at the origins of the concept and categorization of race. The racial imagination developed in Western Europe and was carried into the colonies, including the United States of America, where it was developed even further. Anti-racism also developed in these regions and yet, has not been as successful. Developing a new vocabulary of the major concepts and relationships that make up the topic of anti-racism should help. Scriptures from many faith traditions, positive peace, and alternatives to violence community projects along with the research studies and resources of anti-racism scholars provide the word stock. My goal is to help individuals, faith groups, and communities including libraries and information institutions adapt their anti-racist strategies to build inclusive communities, provide "anti-racist" intellectual access, and "just library service." My research is disseminated through diverse events such as adult education classes and workshops to faith-based, civic, and community groups, besides journal articles, and peer-reviewed conferences.

Funding from the Presbyterian Women of the Synod of Southern California and Hawaii and the Center for Applied Research on Human Services, San Jose State University is gratefully acknowledged and helped in ADL development.

About the Collections (in alphabetical order)

Collections of information resources are the major organizing principle in the Anti-racism Digital Library. There are two types of collections. Themed collections are subject (topical) collections. Community Collections are the creative contents and products of or representative of a group of people.

Themed Collections

The **American Identity Collection** brings together the narratives of individuals and groups who are claiming and carving their identity as Americans without racial tones. Language, culture, ethnicity, faith, art, music, geographic and national origins (including multiple land origins), class (economic, educational, social), and various occupational and other professional group memberships are shown to have far more meaning than racial categories.

The **Anti-racist Identity Collection** brings together resources that highlight the key characteristics of an anti-racist identity such as Inclusivity, Inter-faith Dialogue, Solidarity, Witness-bearing (Christian). It includes exercises and other tools to help the move away from a racial imagination by eliminating the concept of race that is based on skin color and phenotypic variations and using elements of faith in its place.

The **Christian Imagination Collection** brings together resources that can be used to engage people and communities to embody Jesus' way of compassion and justice for our world grounded in the belief that all humanity is made *imago dei* (image of God).

The **Invisible Intersectionality Collection** brings together resources that show the role of intersectional in how people are marginalized, discriminated and oppressed. Individuals and groups often have shared or overlapping interests and characteristics beyond 'race' or ethnicity such as class, gender, and more. Often those who are oppressed, marginalized and discriminated are at the intersection of gender, class and race/ethnicity. This is intersectionality. It is often invisible.

The **Racial Imagination Collection** brings together resources that highlight the powerful grip and influence race plays in our individual and collective consciousness, ways of thinking, behaving, and acting. Items here can be used to raise questions about the continued usefulness and validity of categorizing people into different races when there is only one human race.

The **Reclaiming Ourselves Collection** documents the stories of a movement that is gaining currency and strength as individuals and groups reclaim their human dignity

Community Collections

The **Presbyterian Women (PW) Collection** includes all the documents related to their Anti-racism efforts from committee reports and visions to toolkits, presentations, and training guides. PW has been an anti-racist organization for a very long time. Only selective documents released after 2000 are included here.

The **PC (USA) Intercultural Church Vision Collection** includes the Confessions, Reflections, Vision statements, Policy statements, Reports and Tools from pastors, church leaders, committees, and the General Assembly of the PC (U.S.A). Three confessions, the 2016 Vision statements, anti-racist policies and reports presented at GA 222 are included. Short contemplative pieces by pastors in the Presbytery of Los Ranchos are also included here. All of the anti-racism related overtures that were passed at GA 223 GA 223 PC(USA) have been compiled into a single document: Anti-racism Related Overtures at GA 223. .

Invitation to Join the ADL:

- **Add a link** to the library from your church/group website, social media, LibGuide, Syllabus, etc.
- **Use** the library to teach Spiritual Formation, Information Literacy, Anti-racism Literacy;
- **Catalog** electronic resources
- **Suggest** and **Contribute** resources;
- **Collaborate** on the development
- Help improve the user experience;
- Schedule a talk or training;
- Become a **Sponsor/Registered User**

For more information about the digital library, contact Anita Coleman, email: dranitacoleman@gmail.com

Anti-racism – Glossary of Terms

The glossary is meant to help in the development of a strong personal anti-racist identity for people, groups, and organizations. Key behaviors, actions, beliefs, roles, values, laws, and some historical events and movements are included. References and sources cited here may be found in most cases in the Anti-racism Digital Library or by doing a Google search. GA 223 PC(USA) references can be found in one single document, Anti-racism Related Overtures at GA 223 in the Anti-racism Digital Library. .

Advocacy (behavior, action): To publicly support a policy or cause and to advocate for its legal adoption and use. Christian political advocacy is a specific anti-racism behavior and a key part of Christian discipleship and anti-racist identity - as advocate. Anti-racism advocacy is not limited to those who profess the Christian faith although they have a centuries long legacy through Christian institutions and organization, missions, and social justice as it may also be called, in abolition, civil rights, prisoner rehabilitation, immigration issues, healthcare, education and more. Activism, Mission, Solidarity, Reparation and Witness-bearing are also related forms of Christian anti-racism.

Affirmative action (law): Policy that strives for increased minority enrollment, activity, or membership, often with the intention of diversifying a certain environment such as a school or workplace.

Ally (role): is a member of an oppressor group who works to end a form of oppression which gives him or her privilege. **Allyship** is a process. Everyone has a lot to learn. Allyship involves a lot of listening. Being an ally is not an identity but rather an ongoing and lifelong process that involves a lot of work. That is why, sometimes, you will hear anti-racists say they're 'doing ally work' or 'acting in solidarity.'

Alternative Dispute Resolution: Any method of resolving disputes without going through the public court system. Arbitration and mediation are the two major forms of ADR.

Ambiguity (belief, value): An emerging quality of visible identity characteristics favored by some.

Anti-racism: Is some form of focused and sustained action, that involves a mix of peoples and groups (i.e. they come from different cultures, faiths, speak diverse languages, etc. in short, intercultural, interfaith, multi-lingual, inter-class, and inter-abled) with the intent to change a system or an institutional policy, practice, or procedure which has racist effects. Anti-racism is also a set of beliefs, behaviors, actions, values, and movements. Christian anti-racism is transformative and integrative. It stands on the side of the poor, vulnerable, the marginalized, oppressed and critiques the state (government), empire, colonialism, capitalism, materialism, militarism (violence), structures of power and privilege and how they play out in society. It acts with intention to change injustices. See also **Bystander Anti-racism**.

Anti-racist identity: The anti-racist person continuously works to share power, uncover and eliminate prejudice that is implicit as well as unconscious and conscious bias, and is aware of privilege.

Anti-racism Education / Anti-racism in Education / Anti-racism Training: A distinction can be made between anti-racism education and its use in education (or other areas of practice and theory such as spiritual formation) versus anti-racism training. Anti-racism education helps us understand the source and consequences of racism as well as our own role in continuing racism or transforming it by our choice of action or strategy. Training gives specific skills – e.g. movement building, how to advocate to local elected officials, how to have conversations on difficult topics in churches. Some best practices for teaching anti-racism education are: 1) Teaching about racialization, not just race whereby learners are equipped with tools to recognize, engage, challenge the reconstructions of racial identities, ideologies and hierarchies as well as issues that racialized (welfare, domestic violence, housing). 2) Teaching about more than difference or stereotypes. It is a pedagogy that directions its attention toward the disruption of white supremacy as a social system. 3) illuminating how racism and racialization shape and are shaped by schools. Thus, anti-racist teaching concerns itself with the sites of pedagogy that matter to those it seeks to hail in the classroom. 4) Articulating, making visible, and teaching how different communities have been racialized differently – Euro-Americans, Native Americans, African Americans, Asian Americans, Hispanics, and more recently people of Muslim and Hinduism faith/origins. 5) Joins in the key conflicts of the day by having a strong presence (e.g. advocacy, activism, charity, solidarity, truth-telling, witnessing).

Anti-racism identity: The anti-racist person continuously works to share power, uncover and eliminate prejudice that is implicit, unconscious and conscious bias, and is aware of privilege and divests from it, when it contributes to injustice.

Beloved Community: The biblical notion of creating a community in which people are accepted, loved, and treated as they need to be treated. Used by Martin Luther King, Jr. Source: Catherine Meeks, A Beloved Community: Christian churches can address racism through spiritual formation.

Bias: A strong tendency to prefer one thing or person. Bias has become synonymous with prejudice, which is unfair liking or disliking and may be based on skin color, sex, religion, etc. **Implicit bias**, an innate bias against anything that is different from us, is built into the amygdala, a part of our brain.

Bicultural education: Pedagogical approach that encourages retention of a child's original or family culture.

Binary paradigm of race: The pattern of framing race issues in terms of two categories: Black and white. Society though has become more diverse. To build an equitable society we need acknowledge we're one human race, separated socially into an unequal hierarchy of many races.

Biological view of race: Once popular view that humanity is divided into four or five major groups, corresponding to objective and real physical differences.

Black: Refers to a person of African descent, who could be from anywhere in the world and of any nationality or cultural identity. Source: PW/Horizons Stylesheet Addendum, Bias Free Guidelines. The label 'black' is sometimes preferred by African Americans for purposes of self-confidence, political identity and solidarity.

Blaxican: A person of mixed heritage that includes Africa, United States of America and Mexico. Walter Thompson-Hernandez, the child of an African-American father and a non-black Mexican mother, started the Blaxican Instagram page as an academic research project for the University of South Carolina, but found himself personally drawn to the project to understand the complexities of race and ethnicity in a country that often sees both as one and the same thing.

Bystander Anti-racism: Is an anti-racism behavior that aims to shift social norms toward intolerance of everyday racism. It appears to displace race and challenge racism. The problem with bystander anti-racism is that it constructs racist acts as "deviant" i.e. casual racism. It is not engaging with the deeper injustices or halting white dominance or supremacy. Also, bystander anti-racism is seen as over-reaction if a member of the same ethnic group who is the racism target engages in it. So it tends to reinforce or center whiteness in anti-racism and continues the property interest in whiteness i.e. white skin, white identity are economically and otherwise valuable.

Call to context: This is the belief that social relations and truth require close attention to history, particularity, and individual experience.

Class: A category usually used to divide members of society into groups in terms of their economic status. The American Heritage Dictionary defines it as a social stratum whose members share certain economic, social, or cultural characteristics." Source: 223rd General Assembly, PC(USA).

Colorblindness: The idea of "I don't see color, I treat all people alike." It is a liberal racism stance that acknowledges the existence of different skin colors and color differences but often refuses to admit or recognize that our society values and places the skin colors on a hierarchy. It trivializes the social lived experience of skin color and adopts the mantra: All colors are beautiful. See also **Property Interest in Whiteness**.

Color imagery: Words, texts, and television images that associate skin color with traits such as innocence, criminality, or physical beauty.

Color labels: Skin colors are used to categorize and describe humans. Skin color matters in our society as it is a signifier loaded with identity and value. People are judged by the basis of their skin color and we think nothing of describing others by using their skin color labels. E.g. Blacks, People of Color, Whites. But blackness, color, whiteness are all constructed and they are not monoliths. It is a part of lived experience that people are from specific places, geographies, have different languages and other factors that are expressions of diversities and particularities within them such as Jamaican not African American, and statements like "But I'm not white ... black .. woman of color, etc." Skin color labels that arise out of identity politics especially are a technique for increasing political power by building group identity and cross-cultural solidarity. But grouping people as whites or blacks, or whites vs. people of color, or whites vs. non-whites also perpetuates discriminatory codes which give pre-eminence to skin color over other meaningful markers. Additionally, they cause despair, disunity, even bias. They don't help end racism. This is why the focus of transformative and integrative anti-racism is on increasing racial equity and ending injustices by celebrating the *imago dei* of humanity.

Colorism: The preference for lighter colored skin. When combined with color imagery, much of the symbolism and metaphors in Christian faith, English and American literature, and traditions contribute to myths such as: Light skin must be shielded from the sun; dark bodies flourish in the sun.

Collaborative Advocacy: Is a process-based tool for bringing about social change and justice. For example, the Georgia Appleseed Center for Law and Justice is using it to reduce the likelihood of harm in future law enforcement community relations. The process looks like this: 1) Legal research and fact-finding with stakeholder interviews to determine if change is necessary; 2) Disseminate findings; 3) Advocate with tools such as: 3.1. Meetings: e.g. Meet with key decision-makers and issue Call to Action, Form Allies and Coalitions; Public education and outreach; 3.2. Legislative Advocacy; ; case-studies and best practices/replication; 3.3. Local change initiatives; 3.4. Comments on proposed rules and testimony: 3.5. Media: Op Eds; Quotes; Blogging and other social media; 3.6. Pilot projects.

Compassion: An observable behavior towards different others. Altruism, empathy, sympathy, pity, concern for the suffering of others are hall-marks of Christian compassion and discipleship.

Concealable stigmas: A concept from Psychology arising from private-public schematization where people have distinct selves in private and public – e.g. gay males in professional settings; blacks who pass as whites. Concealable stigmas cause psychological distress and poor health.

Cosmopolitanism: Is from the Greek word, *kosmopolites,* which means "a citizen of the world." It is also a viewpoint and ethical stance about the world. Differences and boundaries are redefined on the basis of an awareness of sameness, in principle, of others. All humans belong to a single community based on shared morality.

Community: Is generally a group of people who interact with one another (e.g. friends), geography (e.g. city), shared beliefs, values, and behaviors (e.g. church).

Critical legal studies: Legal movement that challenged liberalism from the Left, denying that law was neutral, that every case had a single correct answer, and that rights were of vital importance.

Critical race theory: Is a movement, a theory and also a book, by Ricardo Delgado and Jean Stefancic. 2001. *Critical Race Theory: An Introduction.* New York University Press. Some of the tenets of critical race theory are: Race is a social construction; Endemic racism; Voices of Color;

Critique of rights: Critical legal studies position that rights are alienating, ephemeral, and much less useful than most people think.

Cross-cultural: Involving two or more cultures, relates to difference cultures, or compares them.

Culture: Sociologists define culture as the values, beliefs, behavior, and material objects that constitute a people's way of life. It goes beyond race and ethnicity. It includes individual and group characteristics such as age, gender, sexual orientation, disability, religion, income level, education, geographical location, profession, music, food, dance, games, and more. Some related words and concepts follow.

Cultural appropriation: Borrowing from another culture and using another culture (usually marginalized) in disrespectful ways – e.g. sports mascots depicting Native Americans.

Cultural competence: Also known as intercultural competence. This is the ability to interact with people of all cultures to ensure that the needs of all community members are met; emerging from health sciences, cultural competence is respectful and responsive attention to the health beliefs and practices, cultural and linguistic needs, of diverse groups. It is also a dynamic process, and evolves in a continuum.

Culturally humble organization: The policies and practices of an organization, its values and mores, which enable that organization and individuals in the organization to interact effectively in an intercultural environment: assessing culture, valuing and managing the dynamics of difference, adapting to difference, and institutionalizing cultural knowledge. Cultural humility is a "way of being" that is reflected in the way an organization treats its members, its employees, its clients, and its community. Source: GA 223, PC(USA), 2018.

Cultural humility: The "ability to maintain an interpersonal stance that is other-oriented (or open to the other) in relation to aspects of cultural identity that are most important to the [person]." The Christian practice of this is explored by Sera Chung, Cultural Humility, Truths, Translation, and Generous Listening, in *Horizons,* May/June 2016.

Cultural identity: Is the identity or feeling of belonging to a group. It is a person's self-perception, self-conception, and sense of belonging to a group. The modern nation state is the framework for external cultural realities which then influence the unique internal cultural realities of people living in that nation. The development of the Internet, World Wide Web and social media have had a profound influence on the cultural identity of Millennials as well as the categorizations of identity itself. Some aspects of cultural identity are: ancestry, nationality (e.g. American, Chinese, Indian), locality (where one was born, grew up), generation (Baby Boomers, Baby Busters, Millennials), social class (aristocracy, rich, middle-class, poor), religion, language, and more. The preservation of cultural identity based upon difference may be a divisive force in society, while cosmopolitanism can lead to a sense of shared citizenship.

Differential racialization: The process by which racial and ethnic groups are viewed and treated differently by a mainstream society that values white supremacy.

Discourse: Formal, extensive, oral or written treatment of a subject; the way we speak about something.

Diversity: Diversity is the state of different things, and it is different from race or culture or ethnicity. Diversity is a gift from God. There are many types of human diversity: Ideological and intellectual, cultural, physical, etc. The Episcopal church has developed a diversity wheel for its anti-racism training. The wheel identifies the major categories of attributes that individuals have that can differentiate them from other individuals. In the inner wheel are: Age, Race/Ethnicity, Gender Identity/Expression, Gender, National Origin, Sexual Orientation, Mental/Physical Ability. The outer wheel has: Family, Organizational Role, Language and Communication Skills, Income, Religion, Appearance, Work Experience, Education, Political Belief.

Doctrine of Discovery: This is a reference to the Papal Bull "Inter Caetera," issued by Pope Alexander VI on May 4, 1493. It stated that any land not inhabited by Christians was available to be "discovered," claimed, and exploited by Christian rulers and that "the Catholic faith and the Christian religion be exalted and be everywhere increased and spread, that the health of souls be cared for and that barbarous nations be overthrown and brought to the faith itself."

Dominant aggressor: Borrowed from laws about domestic violence, the dominant aggressor is the person determined to be the most significant, rather than the first, aggressor.

Dominant hierarchies: Dominance hierarchies exist in numerous social species, and rank in such hierarchies can dramatically influence the quality of an individual's life.—Robert Sapolsky

Empathy: Is the ability to understand and share the feelings of another and is at the heart of the many struggles for justice.

Environmental justice: First articulated by Dr. Robert Bullard to denote the movement to resolve the problems created by the confluence of environmental destruction, racism, and poverty. Source: 223rd GA, PC(USA), 2018.

Environmental racism: First coined by the Reverend Benjamin Chavis in 1981, and used to describe the disproportionate burden of environmental problems that people of color experience. In his landmark national study, *Toxic Waste and Race in the United States*, he showed statistically that in the United States people of color are more likely to live in areas more exposed to pollutants in the air, ground, and water. Also, it has been found that environmental catastrophes, such as floods, hurricanes, and earthquakes, disproportionately impact people of color because these communities are more likely to live in substandard housing and within floodplains; and people of color generally have fewer resources to escape environmental disasters. E.g. Hurricane Harvey. Source: 223rd GA, PC(USA), 2018.

Epistemic racism: Epistemology refers to the study of knowledge, exploring questions such as how knowledge is acquired and what assumptions are made in the historical development of knowledge. This area of inquiry is critical to understanding racism because the dominance of western knowledge systems produces and promotes beliefs about racialized cultures as inferior to western culture. For Indigenous people, these knowledge systems played a key and relentless role in their portrayal as primitive or noble savages who were less evolved than Europeans. 'Civilization' was thus legitimated as an obligation of the colonial group. Source: Understanding Racism by Charlotte Reading.

Essentialism: The search for the unique essence of a group, the proper unit, or atom, of social analysis and change. The question, do all oppressed people have something in common lies at the heart of the Essentialism/Antiessentialism debate.

Essentialism has a political dimension. Essentialism is paring something down until the heart of the matter stands alone.

Ethnic group: A group socially defined on the basis of cultural characteristics of diverse types such as language, religion, kinship organization, dress, and mannerism, or any other set of criteria deemed relevant to the actors concerned. Source: Merrill-Sands, D., Holvino, and Cumming. Working with Diversity, Working Paper, No. 11, Center for Gender in Organizations, Simmons Graduate School of Management, MA, USA: 2000

Ethnicity: Is a shared cultural heritage. Members of an ethnic category have common ancestors, language, or religion that, together confer a distinct social identity. According to the PW/Horizons Stylesheet Addendum, Bias Free Guidelines: Ethnicity is ancestry, history or geographical origin shared by a group of people; while race refers to physical characteristics shared by a group of people. Both of these are social constructs; genetic differences do not support these labels

Euro-Americans: People whose recent origins are in the continent of Europe. **Euro-centricism** is the tendency to interpret the world in terms of European values and perspectives and the belief that they are superior.

Exceptionalism: A belief that a particular group's history justifies treating it as unique. American exceptionalism, nationalism, patriotism, and jingoism are often conflated.

Exceptionality: A term in multicultural education which is applied to students with specialized needs or disabilities.

False consciousness: A phenomenon in which oppressed people internalize and identify with attitudes and ideology of the controlling class.

Gender Equality: Women and men have equal conditions for realizing their full human rights and potential to contribute to national, political, economic, social, and cultural development and to benefit equally from the results, not by becoming the same, but by correcting the systemic nature of inequality. Source: Association of Women's Rights in Development.

Golden Rule: Do unto others as you would like them to do to you. In the Bible, this is the Parable of the Good Samaritan. The Rev. Dr. Martin Luther King, Jr. explained it thus: The man was good because he made concern for others the first law of his life.

Hegemony: Domination by the ruling class, and unconscious acceptance of that state of affairs.

Hypodescent: "One-drop rule" that holds that anyone with any degree of discernible African ancestry is black.

Imago Dei: It is Latin for God's image and reflects the Christian belief that all humanity is created in God's image; it is a problematic term that goes beyond physical, bodily form to include certainly spirituality, character and attributes (Genesis 1: 26-27 and 9:6). It is a key term for understanding the divine-human relationship in biblical thought. Source: Harper Collins Bible Dictionary by Paul Achtemeier. Revised edition. 1996.

Immigrant analogy: A belief that racialized minority groups, especially Latinx and Asians, will follow the same path of assimilation as white European ethnics.

The **Immigration** and Naturalization **Act of 1965**: Also known as the Hart-Celler Act, abolished an earlier quota system based on national origin and established a new **immigration** policy based on reuniting **immigrant** families and attracting skilled labor to the United States.

Inclusion: The Rev. Dr. Eric Law in the book "Inclusion: Making Room for God's Grace" (2000, Chalice Press) defines inclusion as a Christian ministry. Inclusion is a process and is much more complicated than exclusion, which is fairly simple and easier to define with regards to people. We often know the kinds of people we don't want to include in our groups or communities and how to set up the boundaries to keep them outside. Once we reject them, we don't have to deal with them. Inclusion, on the other hand, is much more complicated. "Inclusion involves a great deal of thinking and listening when we take into consideration others' experience, history, feelings, and so forth. Inclusion requires time and energy to follow up after a person or a group has been physically included. Once a group is embraced in our circle, we have to live with its members for an unspecified period of time." (p. 7)

Information institutions: Are cultural heritage institutions such as archives, libraries, museums and knowledge structures for intellectual access such as the library catalog, electronic indexes and databases, classification schemes, authority lists, subject headings and thesauri.

Inter-able: Inclusive of people of varying levels of abilities (intellectual, cognitive, or physical disabilities, legally blind).

Intercultural: Respecting and embracing different cultures or cultural identities within a society or nation, holding each as equally valuable to and influential upon the members of society. An intercultural church treasures the different cultural contexts that God gives to different individuals and communities and values diverse expressions of practicing the faith. It offers a positive vision of the whole community, together in its difference. It encourages a healthy critique of each other's points of view, and it values the give and take of respectful relationships. It also takes steps to become a multilingual community. Source: GA 223, PC(USA), 2018.

Intercultural Church Movement: Igniting the intercultural vision in the church is a radical transformation calling all of us to change. The movement inspires Presbyterians to: *I-Interact* and build deep relationships with people of different races and cultures, *E- Educate* in the areas of cultural humility and intercultural ministry, and *I- Involve* ourselves in intercultural coalitions to ignite the vision for intercultural ministries in the church in this new era. Source: GA 223, PC(USA), 2018.

Intercultural Coalitions: Individuals of different races and cultures who join together in groups as allies, advocates, and partners, learning from one another, strategizing and taking action to disrupt racism, actively resisting white privilege, challenging social and historical inequalities that permeate institutions, and joining together in the vision of becoming God's intercultural community. Source: GA 223, PC(USA), 2018.

Interest convergence: Thesis pioneered by Derrick Bell that the majority group tolerates advances for racial justice only when it suits its interest to do so.

Internalized racism: Victims of racism internalize it by developing ideas, beliefs, and behaviors that support or collude with white supremacy, are rewarded for supporting it or punished when they are not. This is also a system of oppression that must be made conscious and explicit. It affects marginalized communities intra-culturally as well as cross-culturally (e.g. cross-cultural hostility) as they struggle against individual and group histories of domination.

Intersectionality: The belief that individuals and classes often have shared or overlapping interests or traits. The experience of the interconnected nature of race, gender, class, ethnicity, etc. (cultural and social), and the way they are imbedded within existing systems, such that they define how one is valued. The reality for people who suffer not only from one form of bias, but also experience a range of other forms of oppression. For instance, most women of color experience discrimination not only because of their race but also because of their gender; in other words, women of color live the intersection of gender and race discrimination.

107

Kingdom of God: In Christian theology, this is the reign of God, or the realm over which God rules or will rule. According to the synoptic Gospels, the term does constitute a central feature of Jesus' proclamation to his contemporaries. Source: Harper Collins Bible Dictionary by Paul Achtemeier. Revised edition. 1996.

Kin-dom of God: Ada Maria Isasi-Diaz is generally credited with coining this term; and the story is that she may have heard it from her friend Sister Georgine Wilson, O.S.F. In "Kin-dom of God: A Mujerista Proposal," Ada Maria Isasi-Diaz challenges the traditional interpretation of the scriptural view of a Kingdom of God as a metaphor for a coming world order. Isasi -Diaz interprets this idea as reflective of the dominant, often oppressive cultural experience of societies during Biblical times and the historical view of Kingdom suggests a form of inclusion in which groups of people lived together with same beliefs and culture, that is quite contrary to our current understanding of kingdom. So she proposes the "kin-dom" of God borrowing from Latin culture's pre-eminent value of family, and leaning into Jesus' inclusion of his disciples and followers as his family, his kin.

Legal realism: Early-twentieth-century forerunner of critical legal studies, which disavowed mechanical jurisprudence in favor of social science, politics, and policy judgment.

Merit: Individual worthiness; critical race scholars question the view that people may be ranked by merit and that distribution of benefits is rational and just.

Meritocracy: A deeply held American value, a political philosophy and a group of skilled, educated, talented people who hold power and enjoy the good things of life on the basis of their talent, efforts, achievement, and skill rather than other qualities such as race or gender.

Micro aggression: Stunning small encounter with racism, usually unnoticed by members of the dominant or majority group.

Minorities: This term is no longer used although a legal definition still exists; minorities are generally a distinctive group of society who are less numerous and have lesser social, economic, legal and other forms of power than the majority group. They have two major characteristics: First, they share a distinctive identity. Second is subordination. Minorities tend to have lesser income, lower occupational prestige, and more limited schooling than their counterparts in the majority. Socio-economic class, race, and ethnicity, as well as gender, are not mutually exclusive issues but are overlapping and reinforcing dimensions of social stratification.

Model minority myth: The idea that Asian Americans are hard-working, intelligent, successful and that other groups should emulate them. This myth has been widely used to denigrate other non-whites since the nineteen sixties.

Multicultural education: Refers to any form of education or teaching that incorporates the histories, texts, values, beliefs, and perspectives of people from many different cultural backgrounds. At the classroom level, for example, teachers may modify or incorporate lessons to reflect the cultural diversity of the students in a particular class. In many cases, "culture" is defined in the broadest possible sense, encompassing race, ethnicity, nationality, language, religion, class, gender, sexual orientation, and "exceptionality," a term applied to students with specialized needs or disabilities. Generally speaking, multicultural education is predicated on the principle of educational equity for all students, regardless of culture, and it strives to remove barriers to educational opportunities and success for students from different cultural backgrounds.

Multiculturism: "Multiculturalism means more than racial balance and inclusion. All members of the community must be competent to communicate with each other for an effective multicultural process... The goals of multicultural competency are increased understanding, respectful communication, and full inclusion of all people, not cultural competence by itself." From, **Uprooting Racism**, Paul Kivel, 2002, p. 226.

Multiple consciousness: Ability of people of color to perceive something in two or more ways, for example as a way a member of his or her group would see it and also as a white person would. (Dubois' Double Consciousness)

Mutual invitation: Is a process for group dialogue articulated by Eric Law in his book **T***he Wolf Shall Dwell with the Lamb: A Spirituality for Leadership in a Multicultural Community* (1993, Chalice Press). Here's how the process flows: The leader or a designated person will share first. After that person has spoken, he or she then invites another to share; it does not need to be the person next to you. After the next person has spoken, that person is given the privilege to invite another to share. If you are not ready to share yet, say "I pass for now" and we will invite [you to share later on]. If you don't want to say anything at all, simply say "pass" and proceed to invite another to share. We will do this until everyone has been invited. Mutual invitation is an useful technique for courageous conversations and bold talks on polarizing topics.

Nationalism: Feelings of patriotism, loyalty and devotion to a nation; especially. See also **Racist nationalism.**

Naturalization: Is the legal process of admitting a foreigner to the citizenship of a country; in Biology it is the introduction of a plant or animal to a region where it is not indigenous. In gardening (horticulture), many gardeners use naturalization as a plant propagation technique (e.g. bulbs like daffodils) to create natural, informal looking gardens.

Non-violence / Non-violent resistance: One of the most powerful tools for anti-racism. Nonviolent campaigns have four basic steps: fact-collection to determine if injustices exist, negotiation, self-purification, and direct action.

Normative: Of, pertaining to, or based on a norm, especially one regarded as broad or universal. Normal.

Oppression: Racism affects different groups, and even sub-groups (e.g. black men vs. black women) differently. Therefore, it makes sense to acknowledge different types of oppression experienced as a part of racism. These include exploitation, marginalization, powerlessness, cultural imperialism, and violence.

Paradigm: Reigning system of belief in a discipline that controls what is seen as possible, relevant, and valid.

People Groups: Rather than use skin color labels, the golden rule for describing other people is to ask them how they would like to be described and then use that. This does not mean that you must be color-blind; rather, it means respecting the whole person. There are many vocabularies and thesauri for naming and labeling people. Some of them are: *Library of Congress Demographic Group Terms* (2015) (LCGDT) for generic and cultural people groups; *Library of Congress Subject Headings* (LCSH) for even more generic labels and terms; ATLA *Thesaurus of Religious Occupational Terms* (TROT) for professional roles, titles, and other terms for people in the field of Religion. Similar vocabularies exist for educators, medical professions, etc. See also PW Horizons / Bias Free Guidelines.

People of Color: The 223rd General Assembly (June 2018) of the PC(USA) approved an overture to change the name of the Advocacy Committee for Racial Ethnic concerns to the Racial Equity Advocacy Committee. As part of this overture and at the request of the Committee the GA also approved to "Direct all six agencies of the PC(USA) to move toward changing "racial ethnic people" to "people of color" in all documents, parlance, and programs from this point forward." Part of the rationale comes "from the 222nd General Assembly (2016), people of color must be the ones to name themselves, and it is always most appropriate to ask individuals how they prefer to identify. Language is ever evolving, and this terminology must be revisited regularly and appropriate naming determined by people of color themselves." **Variation: Women of Color.**

Pluralism: Is a social state in which racial and ethnic minorities are distinct but have social parity. The Pluralism Project by Diana Eck and others at Harvard Divinity School's Andover Harvard Theological Library offers more nuanced definitions as well as resources, research, and glossary.

Prejudice: A pre-judgement drawn in the absence of evidence and held in the face of evidence that contradicts it. Source: GA 223, PC(USA), 2018.

Principle of involuntary sacrifice: The notion that costs of civil rights advances are always placed on blacks or low-income whites.

Privilege: Unearned benefits that accrue to a group based on their location in a social hierarchy. White (skin) privilege is a common, pernicious one but there are other privileges based on economic class, race, education, ethnicity, and culture.

Property interest in whiteness: The idea that white skin and identity are economically valuable. A classic paper is by Cheryl Harris, *Whiteness as Property*. (Available in the Anti-racism Digital Library.)

Race: According to John J. Macionis, in his undergraduate college course textbook, ***Sociology*** (6th edition, Prentice-Hall, 1997): "A race is a category composed of people who share biologically transmitted traits that members of a society deem socially significant. ... although we readily distinguish "black" and "white" people, research confirms that our population is genetically mixed... In short, no matter what people may think, race is no black-and-white issue." (page 320). Race is based on phenotype (skeletal structure, hair texture, skin tone) or ancestry (lineage, including tribal and national allegiances).

Racial capitalism: Deriving social and economic value from racial identity. Source: Cedric Robinson, Black Marxism.

Racial ethnic: In the Presbyterian Church (U.S.A.), the double adjective racial ethnic used to be the preferred term for **people of color**. The 223rd assembly (2018) changed that. The 199th General Assembly (1987) defined a racial ethnic group as "a group that defines itself and is defined by others as being phenotypically or culturally divergent from the dominant White American group. And most crucial is the fact the racial ethnic group has held and continues to hold ascribed and unequal states in participation and representation in most, if not all major institutions of American society."

Racial equity: Is key to justice and a goal of anti-racism. In an ideal situation a society's markets and institutions will function well for all people. The data does not support this. Thus, in order to improve racial equity we must achieve greater social justice. This means meeting individual people where they are, and when resources are limited as they often are, ensuring that the same kind of justice is experienced. Popular images of racial equity and justice are: leveling the playing field which is controversial, removing barriers, and the popular scales of justice. In this last image, imagine the dominant group on one scale and one of the subordinate groups on another in terms of level of educational attainment, number of employed, number of home owners, number of never incarcerated, number of poor, and so on. When the scales are balanced on these and other socio-economic and health indicators, then, racial justice has been achieved.

Racial justice: Is the belief, actions, and movement that there is only one human race; justice is a basic human right for all people, irrespective of skin color, national origin, etc.

Racial justice: Is the belief, actions, and movement that there is only one human race; justice is a basic human right for all people, irrespective of skin color, national origin, etc.

Racial realism: View that racial progress is sporadic and that people of color are doomed to experience only infrequent.

Racialized people, racialized person, racialized group, are recent terms for the outdated and inaccurate terms of 'racial minority,' 'visible minority,' 'person of color' or 'non-White.'

Racialization is the process by which a society or a group creates races; in the USA, the Office of Management and Budget is in charge of the Census race categories which started with Free White Males, Free White Females, All other free persons, and Slaves as a count of property. White has remained the norm even though the definition of who is white has kept changing over the last 200 years. Colored became Negro, Black, and African-American. The Census calls Latino/Hispanic an ethnicity, not a race; in the 2020 Census they tried but failed to add MENA for Middle Eastern and North African people, now considered White, as a separate category. People as well as issues – housing, terrorism, immigration - are racialized. The processes of racialization are fluid, they keep changing, and we live in a racialized society and an increasingly racialized world.

Racism: Power + Racial prejudice = Racism. An ideology that either directly or indirectly asserts that one group, whose own characteristics and markers keep shifting over time, is inherently superior to others. It is a system of privilege and oppression that rests on an understanding of humans as belonging to different races ordered in a hierarchy. People are given different treatment. It can be openly displayed in racial jokes and slurs or hate crimes but it can be more deeply rooted in attitudes, values, and stereotypical beliefs. In some cases, **these beliefs are unconsciously held** and have **become deeply embedded in people, systems and institutions that have evolved over time.** Racism operates at a number of levels, individual, systemic, institutional, and societal, national, international, and these are all connected.
Internalized racism is when racist stereotypes and ideologies lead to feelings of self-doubt, disgust, and disrespect.
Interpersonal racism is dislike or bias against another racial group. See also **Systemic Racism.**

Racist nationalism: Expressions whereby whole other nations are disparaged. Source: 223rd GA PC(USA), 2018.

Reconciliation is the spiritual practice of seeking loving, liberating and life-giving relationship with God and one another, and striving to heal and transform injustice and brokenness in ourselves, our communities, institutions and society. **Racial reconciliation** is a journey towards becoming the **Beloved Community** marked by intentional learning, Bible study, prayer, and spiritual disciplines.

Relational Racism: Relational racism occurs when a person experiences discriminatory behavior from people he/she encounters in his/her daily life (e.g., being followed by sales people in stores; being ignored in a line up when their turn comes; being denied promotion by an employer when others are receiving one for doing less well; and having others avoid close personal contact, particularly in isolated locations or at night). Source: Understanding Racism by Charlotte Reading. **Reparation** is an anti-racism process whereby anti-racists redress a relationships with equity. What Does Anti-racism have to do with equity? By Joy Bailey in *Crossroads Antiracism Organizing and Training.*

Representation (or recognition) is one of the most important elements of anti-racism, used to challenge white supremacy as well as other systems of domination (e.g. patriarchy).

Resilience is an anti-racism strategy and a developmental process. It refers to the ability to bounce back and thrive after negative life situations and traumas; resilience can be built up as a process of adaptation in the face of racialization and racism (i.e. ongoing, continuing injustices and suffering).

Restorative justice: Restorative justice views crime as harm done. It is a theory of justice that emphasizes repairing the harm caused by criminal behavior. It is best accomplished through cooperative processes that include all stakeholders. This can lead to transformation of people, relationships and communities. Restorative justice has deep spiritual roots and is

an anti-racist way to deal with racism and move beyond it too.
Source: Tutorial: Intro to Restorative Justice, available online,
http://restorativejustice.org/

Reverse discrimination: Is also known as reverse racism.
Reverse racism reared its ugly head when some universities
did away with affirmative action quotas because they were
accused of discriminating against whites: "individual blacks
and members of other minority groups began to be given
benefits at the expense of whites who, apart from race, would
have had a superior claim to enjoy them." Many Americans
believe that reverse racism is a significant social problem.

Safe spaces: A safe space is a sanctuary and necessary for
cultivating **resilience**. It may be a physical or cultural space
(e.g. church, classrooms). People are important safe spaces.

Sexism: Refers to gender stereotyping of women and men as
hierarchically ordered (men over women) and also as confined
to limited cultural identities and roles as "masculine" and
"feminine." It is expressed in the exclusion of women from
certain types of employment or leadership roles that are
assumed to be the prerogatives of males. Sexism is expressed
in personal, interpersonal, cultural, economic, legal, and
political terms, and is part of a total social and cultural system.
Source: Rosemary Radford Ruether, *Dictionary of Feminist
Theologies*, Westminster/John Knox. Letty M. Russell and J.
Shannon Clarkson, 1996.

Stereotype: A stereotype is a "social distortion." It is a fixed
notion or conception of a person, group, idea, etc., allowing
for no individuality and no critical judgment of individual
cases. Stereotypes are usually based on false generalizations
about a particular category of people, and are often used to
justify the actions taken against members of that group.

Structural racism: Racism has been institutionalized and is
deeply enculturated in our national life, our systems, our laws,
our culture, our words, images, vocabulary, attitudes, and

preferences. It is sometimes maintained unintentionally by institutions and their structural tools (e.g. library catalogs) .

Systemic Racism: The belief that racism has been institutionalized and is also deeply enculturated in our national life, our systems, our laws, our culture, our words, images, vocabulary, attitudes, and preferences. Institutional and Structural racism are both forms of systemic racism. Even the educational system is tainted with institutional and structural (system wide) racism. Example: European or Western ways of knowing are privileged over others. This is epistemic racism. Environmental racism is another specific type of systemic racism.

Token, Tokenism, Tokenization: Perfunctory or symbolic representation to give minimal appearance of racial equality.

Tolerance: An attitude, an active acceptance of difference, as well as respecting and valuing difference as the norm; tolerance implies that no attempts such as bans are made to silence opposing views (censorship), quell or hide differences.

Transparency phenomenon: Ability of whiteness to disguise itself and become invisible.

White: White Ethnic Americans is a term that gained currency during the 1960s recognizing the visible ethnic heritage and the social disadvantages of white Americans without non-English European ancestry. A 'white' identity can also have more to do with lack of wealth, education, and social power than skin color. The histories of groups previously considered non-white such as Irish and Jews show this. A lack of ethnic identity among young white skin Americans has contributed to the rise of a white identity that is centered on race.

White People and Anti-racism: The 223rd GA PC(USA) identified 8 steps for 'white members' especially to help end racism:

1. **RECOGNITION**—As it happened in John 20:11–18, like Mary Magdalene, we hear our names called and recognize that we are captive to the power of race. We cease denying that race has power in our individual and communal lives.

2. **REPENTANCE**—We acknowledge to ourselves and to others that race has power in our lives and contributes to our white privilege.

3. **RESISTANCE**—We commit ourselves to combating the power of racism in ourselves, in others, in churches, and in institutional life. Because of its long reach in American history, at times we will feel like those who are battling principalities and powers in Ephesians 6:10–20.

4. **RESILIENCE**—We are called to affirm the traditional ways of combating racism while seeking new ways to engage a powerful force that continues to be present in American life and that continues to evolve.

5. **REPARATIONS**—We commit ourselves to doing our part to repair the breaches that have been made through racism, including psychological, spiritual, and economic damage.

6. **RECONCILIATION**—We recognize that we have long benefitted from racism and that in order for reconciliation to take place, we will need to work the first five steps listed above.

7. **RECOVERY**—We receive and commit ourselves to live by a new vision of a humanity created by God to live in love, equity, and justice rather than in the hierarchy and domination of the system of race.

8. **RESONANCE**—We understand and resonate with our own cultural background.

Source: 223rd GA, PC (USA). 11-11 Declare an Imperative for the Reformation of the Presbyterian Church (U.S.A.) in being a Transformative Church in This Intercultural Era. Steps 1–7 are from "Seven Steps for Those Classified as White to Use in Engaging Our Racism" by Nibs Stroupe.

Violence: In Law, violence is the unlawful exercise of physical force or intimidation by the exhibition of such force. But there are many forms of violence that are complicit with racism. Example: Symbolic violence is the nearly worldwide acceptance of European standards of beauty. Source: Matthew

Desmond and Mustafa Emirbayer, What is Racial
Domination? In Du Bois Review, 6:2 (2009) 335–355.

White privilege: The unearned advantages that come to
whites in the system of racial preference. Whites tend to
assume that they are "normal" and that others are "other."
This puts them in the powerful position of defining the world.
The concrete benefits of access to resources and social
rewards and the power to shape the norms and values of
society that whites receive, either consciously or
unconsciously, by virtue of their skin color in a racist society
where those who are considered to be white are the dominant
group. Generally white people who enjoy such privilege do so
without being conscious of it. The sense of whites as non-
raced and others as being racialized perpetuates the assumed
authority of whites to define, and with this assumed authority
whites define everyone (themselves and others) in terms of
themselves. Whites assume the right to make meaning, to
describe, analyze, and define reality. This definition nearly
always places whites and their/our definitions and
understandings at the center; all others are hyphenated or
labeled as other. Source: "Working Definitions" prepared for
antiracism training in the PC(USA). See also *White Privilege*:
Unpacking the Invisible Knapsack" by Peggy Macintosh,
Peace and Freedom Magazine, July/August, 1989, pp. 10-12.
Finally, it must be remembered that white privilege is a system
feature but individuals are beneficiaries.

White supremacy: Often thought to be connected only to
extremist, right-wing hate groups. However, the term white
supremacy is also a specific term for racism. It is a more
accurate descriptor for the reality of the everyday experiences
of people of color. It exists in the overt form of right-wing
white power groups, as well as a form of oppression that is
reproduced by the everyday practices of a well-intentioned
liberal society. For example, skin color that is closer to white
also reaps automatic rewards and privileges. In anti-racism
we must constantly be aware of our own privileges, and divest
from it when we that it is complicit in oppression. Examples

of white supremacy include, **Appeals to colorblindness; Whiteness as the norm.** See also **Oppression.**

Whiteness: Anti-racism scholar and activist Paul Kivel defines whiteness as "a powerful fiction, and enforced by power and violence. Whiteness is a constantly shifting boundary separating those who are entitled to certain benefits from those whose exploitation and vulnerability to violence is justified by their not being white."

Witness bearing (Christianity): In Psychology, bearing witness is a term that refers to sharing our experiences with others, especially communication of traumatic experiences. In an increasingly anxious world fragmented by shifting norms, rising inequalities, and the inability to live with differences, the Christian bears witness to the gospel of Jesus Christ.

X: The 24th alphabet in the English language is also the mark that Old Testament people put on their forehead and also on the doorposts to avoid being smitten by the angel of death. Today, X is being used to signify inclusion. The x in Latinx makes it inclusive to gender nonconforming, gender, non-binary, and gender fluid people, instead of the gender-binary Latino, Latina, and Latin@.

ABOUT THE AUTHORS

Anita Coleman, Ph.D. is a wife, mother, and independent scholar. She is the founder and curator of the Anti-racism Digital Library. Anita has published books and blogs about her faith: *Garden of Grace: A Daybook of Faith and Healing* (30 day devotional on Ephesians); *Casa Charis: A Daybook of Freedom* (31-day devotional on Galatians); *Eyes on Christ: Reflections on Being the People of God in the PC (USA)* (discernment and community building on polarizing issues); *Ocean of Grace:* Two short stories, a few poems, and a reflection; **and** *Path of Grace*, her first diversity and water-wise earth-friendly, read-aloud children's book. Anita serves on the Board of Directors of the Presbyterian Writers Guild and Presbyterian Women, Inc. Her hobbies are digital and drone photography, gardening, and reading.

Stephanie Patterson Morris is a graduate of the Louisville Presbyterian Theological Seminary with certification in Black Church Studies and is currently a doctoral student seeking a Doctor of Management (DM) in Organizational Leadership. She has worked at the national office of the Presbyterian Church (U.S.A.) for 25 years where she is currently Multimedia Associate/Designer for Presbyterian Women in the PC(USA), Inc. Stephanie is also adjunct faculty at Spalding University and the Louisville Education Center of Indiana Wesleyan University. Stephanie is a proud member of Sigma Gamma Rho Sorority, Inc. guided by the principle of "Greater Service, Greater Progress." She is passionate about antiracism and the journey to equality, and enjoys any and everything creative, artistic, electronic and web savvy. Most of all, she loves spending time with her family. Stephanie strives to "walk by faith and not by sight" and acknowledges, "all things are possible through Christ."

Francena Willingham, Ph.D., 1949-2018, was a retired educator, administrator, and college professor. A native of Columbia, South Carolina, Francena at the time of her sudden death in June, was serving on the Board of Directors for Presbyterian Women, Inc. and the South Carolina Federation of Women's & Youth Clubs, Inc. She was an Honorary Life Member by PW of Ladson Presbyterian Church, a **Diamond Life** member of Delta Sigma Theta Sorority, Inc., a *Life* member of both the Girl Scouts and the National Association of Colored Women's Clubs. "Reading books on the antebellum era and African American history," in Francena's own words, was her "drug of choice."

Ash Coleman is a young millennial man, a Certified Public Accountant, gifted with numbers and words. He likes to speak kindly and act gently so that everybody can have justice and live in peace. A movie buff, Ash enjoys video games and likes to draw with pencils.

Marvella Lambright lives in Dayton, Ohio and serves on many PC (USA) boards and commissions, including service on the Board of Directors, Presbyterian Women, Inc. as the Synod Representative from the Synod of the Covenant.

Susan Skoglund is a servant leader who has served in many capacities with Presbyterian Women, Inc. She is the Moderator of the PW of the Synod of Southern California and Hawaii.

Sharon Wakamoto has served in many leadership capacities in her church, Placentia Presbyterian Church, Los Ranchos Presbytery, as well as Presbyterian Women at the Synod and national levels.